ABOUT THE AUTHOR

SHERRYLL KRAIZER has a PhD in education with a specialization in youth at risk. She is the founder and director of the Coalition for Children, a not-for-profit organization for the prevention of interpersonal violence. She is a Special Education Instructional Specialist for the Denver Public Schools and provides expert witness services in bullying and institutional child abuse cases. Kraizer is the author of the Take a Stand: Prevention of Bullying program used in schools throughout North America. She is also the author of *The Safe Child Book*, the Safe Child Program, the Reach, Challenge and Recovery Programs for at-risk youth.

Kraizer has taught and worked with schools for more than twenty-five years developing programs that provide effective, affordable life skills education. Her work is based on the belief that families, schools, and communities need to share the job of positively educating and empowering children to speak up for themselves, to respect themselves and others, and to be powerful advocates for a society that recognizes the value of every child.

Dr. Kraizer is internationally recognized for creating models that maximize community-wide participation in prevention efforts and for her research of program effectiveness, including what methods ensure actual behavioral change associated with reduction of risk. Her materials are translated and used in eighty countries around the world. She lives in Denver with her husband Al and their son Charlie. She can be reached at www.safechild.org.

10 Days *to a* Bully-Proof Child

The Proven Program
to Build Confidence and
Stop Bullies for Good

SHERRYLL KRAIZER, PhD

MARLOWE & COMPANY
NEW YORK

10 DAYS TO A BULLY-PROOF CHILD:
The Proven Program to Build Confidence and Stop Bullies for Good

Copyright © 2007 by Sherryll Kraizer, PhD

Published by
Marlowe & Company
An Imprint of Avalon Publishing Group, Incorporated
245 West 17th Street • 11th Floor
New York, NY 10011-5300

AVALON
publishing group incorporated

Library of Congress Cataloging-in-Publication Data is available

ISBN-13: 978-1-56924-253-7
ISBN-10: 1-56924-253-4

9 8 7 6 5 4 3 2 1

Printed in the United States of America

*For my mom
and
the Graves girls*

ACKNOWLEDGMENTS

Writing a book is really a community effort. I would first like to acknowledge all the children who have shared their experience of being bullied, being bullies, and learning to be advocates for others. What I know about preventing interpersonal violence I learned from them and their parents.

I want to thank the many readers who reviewed the initial manuscript and brought to it their personal perspectives. They understand bullying from many points of view, all of which enriched this book. Eve Eifler, Amy Luce, Celine Marquez, and Suzanne Rougier are all mothers, educators, and wise souls who made sure this book spoke to the real-life situations children face every day!

Thank you equally to the women of my family, who brought multiple generations of insight. Phyllis Graves, my mother and dear, dear friend, thank you for being my champion, for appreciating who I am, and nourishing every wild idea I ever had! Jacque Cooley, Nancy Graves, Cynthia Graves, and Susan Graves, my sisters and friends, who provided key ideas and balance at just the right moments. Melanie and Jennifer Cooley, Megan and Danielle Graves, Kathryn Tindell, Jesica Greek, and Lyndsey Graves, the next generation of young and powerful women, who remind us that what we do every day matters!

Special thanks go to Jane Brody, who brought the idea for this book forward, to my agent, Faith Hamlin, a true champion, and

Katie McHugh, my editor, who brought a new eye to the book and helped shape it to reflect multiple points of view.

Last, but never least, I thank my husband, Al, and son, Charlie, for supporting the work I do, even when it infringes mightily on their time!

If you were bullied or continue to be bullied, this book is ultimately for you. It is never too late to stand up for yourself, to ask for help, and to stand up for others. If as you read this book you have experiences or ideas to share, please do not hesitate to contact me by visiting the Web site www.safechild.org.

CONTENTS

INTRODUCTION

Q: *"My daughter was so eager to start second grade in her new school. All summer, she talked about making new friends, having them over to play, going to their houses. Then, only two weeks into the school year her enthusiasm vanished. Things gradually got worse and her reluctance to go to school evolved into morning headaches. When she began throwing up every morning, I begged her to tell me what was wrong. She told me that she had no friends because one girl in her class had persuaded all the other girls to ignore her. She described how they whispered about her, excluded her on the playground, and dropped cruel notes on her desk. I was heartbroken. I went to the school, hoping her teacher and I could solve the problem, that she could tell me what to do. Instead, the teacher explained that this teasing was just a part of learning to get along, that my daughter needed to be less thin-skinned. I was outraged and went to the principal, hoping he would help, but he referred me back to the teacher. I kept thinking to myself, how could this be?"*
— Suzanne P., *parent of seven-year-old*

SHERRYLL SAYS: *"First and foremost, the school needs to understand that this is not a 'normal' part of growing up. Teasing, exclusion, and gossip are all forms of bullying. They undermine a child's developing sense of self. The school needs to be educated, to recognize how bullying affects the culture of the school. They need to understand that children who do not feel safe cannot* *learn. I recommend that you approach the problem from two different directions. First, work with your daughter on the strategies found here. Build up her interpersonal skills and sense of self. At the same time, approach your school PTA and initiate a discussion about bullying. Bring materials that simply and clearly define the range of behaviors that constitute bullying, the effect it has on children, and schoolwide strategies for creating a culture that does not accept bullying. Ask that the school develop a policy and consistent procedures for preventing and responding to bullying. This is a long-term process, and the more parents and teachers you can engage in supporting development of a schoolwide response, the more positive the environment will be for your daughter."*

If the above situation sounds familiar, you've come to the right place. When parents learn that their child is being bullied, it invokes powerful emotions, including anger, sadness, powerlessness, and confusion. Some want to confront the bullying head-on, right now! Others wonder if their child has brought it on and really does need to "toughen up."

Parents are naturally concerned that their children will be targeted by bullies. They wonder if their kids will tell them if there is a problem. They don't generally know what programs schools have in place to prevent or deal with bullying. They want to strike a balance between being overly protective and leaving kids to solve their own social problems.

I receive e-mails every day from parents describing difficult bullying situations like the above. They don't know what to say to their children that will really make a difference. They may have been unsuccessful in working with the school or community group or the other children and adults involved in the bullying situation. Rarely do parents know what to do to effectively change the situation.

Bullying, unfortunately, has become a part of our culture. The statistics tell us how prevalent it is. The National Association of School Psychologists reports that, at any given time, 25 percent of U.S. students are the targets of bullies, and about 20 percent are engaged in bullying behavior. Now that our country has witnessed several school shootings, we all know that bullying can become serious enough to provoke extreme violence. Yet, many adults and teachers still don't take incidents seriously in their own communities and schools.

The reach of bullying into the future is also long and damaging. Being bullied affects a child's self-esteem, increases anxiety, and can cause profound sadness and depression. Being bullied makes children feel afraid, lonely, isolated, angry, and often physically ill. Children who are chronically bullied begin to live their lives in a state of nervous "alertness," waiting for the next attack. These children can become increasingly withdrawn and unable to fit in socially.

On the other hand, bullies also pay an enormous personal toll. As long as bullies get satisfaction from their behavior, and it is allowed to continue, the bullying will continue and will probably escalate over time. Children who bully are more likely to grow up to bully their partners and their children. They are more likely to exhibit aggressive behavior and to become engaged in delinquency and interpersonal violence.

The pervasiveness of bullying is seen in how easy it is for most of us to remember a specific bullying incident from our past. If you were the target, you remember the panic, the sick feeling, wondering why no one was helping. If you were the bully, you remember the feeling of power and perhaps shame for what you did to others. Maybe you were a bystander. If so, you probably remember the anxiety of not wanting to be the next target, and maybe the guilt you felt for not intervening, even if you didn't know how.

Just as Suzanne (in the opening story) hit a brick wall with her child's school, you may also have experienced the frustration of dealing with a school bureaucracy or neighborhood community that is unwilling to recognize or change the situation. This happens for two important reasons. First, they genuinely do not understand the range of behaviors that constitute bullying or how profoundly damaging it is to children. Second, and probably more importantly, they really have no idea how to stop it. They put up "Bully-free Zone" signs on the walls of the school and hope it works. Beyond that, most adults are not skilled at implementing strategies that prevent or intervene in bullying situations.

If your child has been bullied, you might feel guilty if you blamed or questioned your child's part in the bullying, or if you thought your child might be causing the aggression. Parents often think their children are bullied because they did something to provoke it, or because they don't have adequate social skills. And many of you know all too well the knot in your stomach when you make a fearful child go to school before you have found a way to address the situation.

But bullying does not need to be a pervasive part of our schools and communities. There is ample evidence that bullying can be cut in half just by the implementation of a strong prevention of bullying program in a school. When we add to this active efforts on the part of families and communities to recognize and understand the issues around bullying, to teach children strong interpersonal skills that value and respect individual differences, and to intervene in bullies' behavior and reeducate them so their behavior becomes appropriate, we have the ability to maintain communities that do not have significant bullying problems.

Over the past twenty-five years, I have worked with hundreds of schools and thousands of children throughout North America to combat all types of abuse and interpersonal violence, and have helped families deal with the fallout of such acts. While working with schools to teach prevention of child abuse, I saw more and more examples of schools that were not dealing with serious bullying issues. In researching the effectiveness of the Safe Child Program, I discovered the key elements that build effective prevention skills for children. They are:

1. Age-appropriate explicit instruction
2. Role-play to move from concepts to skills
3. Application of those skills to real-life situations

In 2000, I introduced the Take a Stand Program, a school-based curriculum that educates school personnel, parents, and children about bullying—what it is, how it feels, the effects of bullying on individuals and the school culture, and how to stop it. This behaviorally based program engages schools, parents, and children in the task of creating bully-free communities. I encourage schools and other child-centered institutions to develop real guidelines and consequences that govern acceptable social interaction. Children learn to role-play communication skills and behaviors that stop bullying. They learn to be advocates, to speak up for themselves and others. I have taken the most powerful tools from that program and created this book to help you significantly reduce the likelihood that your child will be a target or a perpetrator of bullying.

While developing good social skills is a lifelong endeavor, there are key concepts and skills that your children can start to develop in just ten days' time. I will provide you with discussion materials and strategies for solving bullying problems. The following introductory chapter explains how to role-play scenarios with your children. On Day 1, you and your child will learn what bullying encompasses, which kids become bullies, and which children are most likely to become the targets of bullies.

On Day 2, you will learn the action steps you should take if you suspect that your child is being bullied or is a bully. There will be many opportunitities to role-play and problem-solve. Day 3 will focus on building empathy and understanding, on respect for individual differences, and on strategies for developing these abilities through activities and cooperative play.

Day 4 will help you develop your child's communication skills, including the tools needed to speak and use body language assertively. Day 5 develops the other side of effective communication: listening, observing, and reading social cues quickly and accurately. Day 6 ties all the previous days' skills together, including recognizing and shifting aggressive and passive behavior patterns, so that your child is able to be assertive and effective. Your kids will get to practice preventing and stopping bullying behaviors.

Day 7 goes beyond communication to provide concrete skills that will enable your child to short-circuit a bully's approach and resist provocation. Day 8 explains how to maintain friendships and overcome troublesome situations in friendships. It also includes some ideas for expanding your child's circle of friends. Day 9 addresses the range of activities that constitute cyber-bullying and how to stay safe in an electronic environment.

Day 10 takes all the previous skills and applies them to advocacy, your child's ability to help others and support a community of kids who do not sit by and let bullying happen. Throughout, it is important to role-play often, to use real situations you or your family has encountered, and to have a good time while you are learning together.

You will see your child's ability to communicate clearly, to behave assertively, and to advocate for himself and others increase every day. You should not be surprised if you see your child role-playing with friends or siblings. Children love to feel in control. They love practicing skills that make them feel successful. While this type of learning never stops, this Take a Stand ten-day program will get your kids firmly grounded in skills that will effectively "bully-proof" them—by preventing bullying in all its forms. I applaud you for picking up this book. You are about to make a real difference in your child's life.

The Take a Stand Role-Play Method

Q: *"I was skeptical about role-playing with my child. I didn't think she would agree to try it, and I sure didn't think she would 'get into it.' Boy, was I surprised! At first she resisted, but once I started actually playing the role of a bully who had pushed her and taken her lunch, she was really 'in the situation.' What I learned just watching her, and playing the scenario out with her, told me everything I needed to know. My daughter actually seemed to shrink as I pretended to push her. She was apologetic and defensive. She made no eye contact, her voice was squeaky, and she really had no idea what to do. This is from a kid who is normally pretty confident. So we went to work. We role-played assertive speaking, body language, and statements, and I watched her confidence go straight up. She took these skills to school, and the bully she had been facing ceased to be a problem for her."*

—Julie K., *mother of six-year-old*

SHERRYLL SAYS: *"I can't tell you how many parents have expressed the same shock that their child, whom they saw as confident and resourceful, had become a target of bullying. But your experience is exactly how role-play is supposed to work. With explicit instruction, modeling, and practice, your child will continue to learn and use the skills you're teaching."*

The Role-Play Method—acting out conflict situations—is the tool that will turn the theories in this book into reality for your children. It is the game you will use to coach your children to better life skills. And it is the way you will find out what your children think about the social problems they encounter and how they actually handle them. Role-play is the primary skill-builder for prevention of bullying, one that I have successfully used with thousands of kids in the Take a Stand anti-bullying program. It's also a lot of fun!

Role-play is practice for life. It's a way of preparing for what we can anticipate. If you were going to your supervisor to discuss a significant problem with a coworker, you'd probably rehearse what you were going to say, or mentally practice how to approach the issue. You'd prepare yourself by thinking through how to respond if your supervisor says this, or that. When you role-play situations with your child, you're helping him or her to build the same skills. Think of it as developing "talking points" so that a bully won't catch your child off guard. Having used this technique not only with my students but also in my own life situations, I know it is the most powerful way to prepare to be effective.

As one parent, a target of bullying in her youth, shared with me, "I know that if someone had role-played with me [as a child], I would have felt so much more empowered and armed, not caught off guard so that I ended up crying or reacting rather than responding. I didn't know how to pause, think of a response, and give it. I also didn't know how to pretend I was feeling something different than what I was actually feeling, in order to protect myself. I was just trying to survive without having any real skills."

The Role-Play Method gives you a window into your child's mind. It enables you to see your child's level of assertiveness, communication skills, and response to threatening or intimidating behavior, and to see his or her progress toward learning more effective strategies for responding to aggressive behavior. It provides a natural forum to assess where your child is currently and then to talk about and act out possible solutions to myriad problems.

DID YOU KNOW?

- Research tells us that children learn concepts by watching, listening, and discussing, but skills can only be learned by doing, by giving children an opportunity to rehearse prevention strategies.
- It is not necessary for programming to be explicit in order to be effective; fear and anxiety levels are lower in programs that teach prevention without talking directly about abusive situations.
- Multiple studies show that the opportunity to apply concepts and turn them into skills through role-play is at the heart of empowering children to prevent abuse.

Why Role-Play Works

Role-play is experiential and thus the most effective avenue for learning that sticks. Actually walking children through specific scenarios and having them practice different responses will give them the skills they need and can really use in everyday situations.

Mastering a skill means that your child learns it in his or her "muscles," so it becomes automatic. For example, consider the difference between understanding the concept of how to ride a bicycle and actually being able to do it. Getting on the bike and experimenting to find balance and control are what bring mastery. And, as we all know, once you learn to ride a bicycle, you never forget. It is part of your "muscle memory."

Learning to speak up for oneself is also a skill learned by doing. When your child is able to say, "Don't do that to me, I don't like it," in a tone of voice that is clear and assertive, while standing up tall and looking directly at you, you will know that role-playing has worked.

Getting Started

Initiating role-play is as simple as asking a "What if . . ." question or responding to your child's "What if . . ." question. For example, say you are having lunch with your child. You might begin with, "I heard that there was a problem in the lunchroom with one of the boys taking other kids' desserts. What would you do if that happened to you?" When your child begins to tell you, suggest, "Show me what you would do, I'll be the kid trying to take your dessert." Play it out. See what resources your child already has.

If your child isn't particularly effective, suggest that you switch roles. Your child is now the bully. You should model or demonstrate sitting up straight, looking the bully in the eye, and clearly saying, "Do not touch my lunch." Then change roles and let your child try it. If he or she gets just partway there, provide positive coaching. For example, "That was pretty good; now look right at me when you say that." Or, "I heard your words, but this time, try saying them a little louder and stronger." When your child is able to respond clearly and in a straightforward manner, acknowledge that success: "Much better! I really got that you meant it!"

Throughout the balance of this book, sample role-play situations that you might want to try will be marked **ROLE-PLAY**. Remember, this is a process. You are learning what skills your child already has and helping him or her to develop new ones. Avoid judging or making an issue over any part of the action, or the value will be lost. Although role-play mimics a confrontation, it should never become a real confrontation between you and your child. It is an opportunity to share ideas, initiate discussion, learn new strategies, and have fun!

The three key elements of role-play are the following:

1. **Speaking:** This includes deciding what you want to say and then saying it in an assertive manner, paying attention to your tone of voice, volume, pitch, clarity, and so on.
2. **Body language:** This includes posture, facial expressions, the distance between the people involved, using your hands to emphasize your point, and the like.
3. **Eye contact:** Communication that is delivered face-to-face and eye-to-eye is the most powerful.

Consistently combining all three of these elements takes time and practice, and you will learn exactly how to do this in the upcoming days. Children usually learn the skills one at a time and then integrate them. For example, your child might get all the words right the first time you role-play but miss the body language. The next time, your child might get the body language and flub the words. Practice and successive approximations, getting a little better every time, are the steps to mastery. By about the third time, most kids will put it all together, and they'll be as tickled as you are at their success. Role-play teaches children how to communicate effectively and consistently, so they can utilize the skills automatically when needed. It is what turns ideas into action. Following are a few role-play scenarios to help you understand how they are used.

> **ROLE-PLAY:** *Hair Pulling*
> Ask your child, "What if one of the girls in your class pulls your hair every time you walk near her? What would you say and do?" Wait to see what your daughter's initial response is before coaching her. Then follow up as needed to include these elements:
> **ACTION 1:** Stop, turn around, and face the girl pulling your hair.

ACTION 2: Remove the girl's hand from your hair.

ACTION 3: Say clearly, with strong body posture and eye contact, "Please stop pulling my hair. I don't like it."

ACTION 4: Then walk away.

DISCUSSION: Be sure to give positive feedback every step of the way if you are actually role-playing this with your child.

ROLE-PLAY: *New Glasses*

Ask your child, "What if one of the kids in your class is making fun of your new glasses, saying something like, 'Four eyes, four eyes, can't see a thing!' What would you say and do?" Your coaching should include teaching your child to:

ACTION 1: Face the child who is making fun of you.

ACTION 2: Say clearly, with strong body posture and eye contact, "That's not a nice thing to say."

ACTION 3: Then walk away.

Remember to be open to other solutions your child might come up with.

ROLE-PLAY: *New Student*

Ask your child, "What if you are with some of your friends and a new kid who has just moved to the United States comes toward your group? One of your friends says to him, 'I don't know where you came from, but you can't play with us.' How do you think that new kid would feel? What could you say or do?" Coach your child to come up with an assertive action. For example:

ACTION 1: Say to your friends, "That's not a very nice way to welcome a new kid. Give him a break." Or "What a mean thing to say! I'd rather hang with him than you guys, if you're going to act that way."

ACTION 2: Walk over to the new kid and invite him to join the group or to participate in another activity.

Children and parents are often surprised how effective a single clear, assertive statement is in stopping a bully. This is because bullies are not expecting to be challenged. It startles them and denies them the satisfaction of intimidating their target. Even if bullies come back to try again, the repeated experience of not having the desired effect will diminish their interest, and they will move on to another child.

Children Take the Lead

Children love to role-play and will rapidly use it as a way to address other concerns they have. This is invaluable for parents. The "What if . . ." questions or scenarios kids suggest reflect their fears, concerns, anxieties, and curiosities. Children hear stories about things that have happened to other children, or they witness something in school or on the playground. They naturally think about what they would do. They want to role-play so they know how to handle a similar situation. —Developing Self

Your daughter might say, "One of the girls at school said she was having a party but she wouldn't be inviting everyone. I don't know if she is going to invite me or not, but what will I do if she says I can't come?"

As parents, we always want to jump in with an answer, but it is more informative and valuable if you ask, "What do you think you would say or do? Do you want to try it with me, and maybe we can figure it out?" →Opportunity to Initiate Role-Play

In role-playing, you might model your daughter, saying, "I know you can't invite everyone, but you shouldn't do it so other people feel bad that they weren't invited."

↳Arouse consciousness and sympathy in others

By eliciting your kids' ideas through role-play, you'll discover how they think, how they solve problems, their concept of how the world and their social groups work, and what they know and don't know about solving interpersonal conflicts. Always look for the skills your child is bringing to these problem-solving "What if . . ." scenarios and acknowledge them. These are the building blocks for future skills.

ROLE-PLAY TEACHES:

- Identification and clarification of ideas and concerns
- Thinking ahead
- Understanding choices and consequences
- Flexibility in a wide range of situations
- Problem solving
- Communication
- Assertiveness
- Resource building
- Ability to ask for help

Role-Play Helps Kids Find Ways to Tell

Children also use "What if . . ." scenarios as a way to tell their parents things that have happened that they don't really want to talk about directly. This is important because many kids resist at all costs telling their parents something that makes them look scared, weak, or mean. It is also a way to get help for a friend. It seems less like tattling, and makes problems easier to talk about. For example, your child might say, "Mom, what would you say if some of my friends were kind of making the little kids miss the bus and blaming it on someone else?"

In the follow-up to this question, you would want to explain that telling about a problem is not tattling, and that you would like to help without making the situation worse. You might role-play your child talking to someone at the school, with or without you. You might decide with your child that this is a situation you should handle with the school directly. Always remember to thank your child for speaking up and for being an advocate for another child. *Acknowledge & validate info*

The other side of this coin is the child who has a strong sense of justice and has a hard time not getting involved in other people's business. The "What if . . ." game can provide lots of opportunities to help your child learn when to step in and when it's really none of his business. For example, you might say, "What if you see a kid flipping his cigarette onto the lawn? You know that's wrong and even dangerous. What could you do other than confront him, especially if you know he's a kid who will find a way to get even?" Brainstorm possibilities such as telling a teacher, talking to you about it later, or just letting it go. Kids with a strong sense of right and wrong need to learn that they can't and shouldn't always respond to what they see.

It takes years to help children who have a strong sense of justice, of right and wrong, learn when and how to advocate or intervene, and when another course is better. I'll discuss this more fully in Day 10, "Advocating for Others."

What If Your Child Doesn't Want to Role-Play?

Every once in a while, a child might resist role-play. If your child responds with, "I don't know" or "I can't do it" to your "What if . . ." question, you will need to assess whether your child really feels insecure and is unable to come up with a response, or just doesn't want to participate. If the problem is uncertainty, very gently coax your child by making suggestions or showing what you might do in the situation. If you can make the role-play silly or laughable, most kids will engage.

If your child's response is, "This is stupid, I don't want to do this," let it go. If your child senses that you are overly invested in the activity, resistance is not uncommon. This is especially true for children over the age of ten. In this instance, look for teachable moments or spontaneous opportunities to bring up role-playing scenarios.

For example, if you see one child push another down on the playground, you might say, "Did you see that? Does that happen a lot at school? What would you do if that happened to you?" If your child doesn't really know, you can bring the subject up again later and suggest, "I was thinking about what I saw on the playground. Can you show me what you would do if that happened to you?" If your child still resists, you might say, "It is important that I know that you can handle lots of different kinds of situations. That way I won't worry about you."

An extension of this applies to older kids. For example, it is totally appropriate, before letting your teenage daughter go to a slumber party, for you to find out whether she could handle a situation in which one of the girls brings out a few cans of beer. This is a high-pressure peer situation, and it is perfectly appropriate to say, "I'm not comfortable letting you go unless I know you could handle this type of situation."

You will be surprised how often life presents opportunities to role-play. Do not hesitate to involve siblings, relatives, or your child's friends. If there is a neighborhood problem that involves several children, you can be explicit. "I understand that Junior is being mean to you guys. Show me what you do if he pushes you." Then role-play responses with each child, or let them role-play with each other. By talking about the problem in a group, they learn that it is a problem for everyone and that they can support one another in not letting it continue.

Using Role-Play with This Book

Role-play scenarios will be provided throughout the ten days. Use them as they are written, or modify them according to your situation or your child's individual skills and needs. Always keep the experience positive, empowering, and fun! Remember that interpersonal skills are learned a little bit at a time, so each step your child takes in the direction of being a clear, powerful, and assertive communicator is important.

SUMMING IT UP

Initiating role-play is as simple as asking a "What if . . ." question or responding to your child's "What if . . ." questions. Through coaching and practice, children learn the skills they need.

The three key elements of role-play are:

1. Speaking assertively, including paying attention to tone of voice, volume, pitch, and clarity
2. Using body language consistent with the speaking, including posture, facial expressions, proximity, and hand motions
3. Making eye contact

Consistently combining all three of these elements takes time, but children gradually learn the skills and put them together. Practice is the key to mastery!

Understanding Bullying: Who Are the Bullies and Targets?

Q: *"My daughter rides the school bus to and from school. There is a boy on the bus that torments the younger kids. He sits next to someone different every day and tells them that he will hurt them if they speak up. Then he proceeds to take their lunch money, their snacks, and their homework. They don't say a word. My daughter is afraid to do or say anything that will bring attention to her. She is afraid she'll be next, but she knows she should do something. What can she do?"*

—Andy W., *parent of eight-year-old*

SHERRYLL SAYS: *"She is right to be cautious. This boy is an opportunistic bully who clearly knows how to intimidate. I would suggest you go to the school with her and talk to the principal. Describe the situation and ask the principal what the school will do to stop this situation. You should also role-play with your daughter what she will do if he sits next to her. Options when the bus is stopped include:*

1. *Getting up and moving to another seat*
2. *Getting up and telling the driver*
3. *Saying loudly, 'No, you cannot have my lunch money!'*
4. *Telling her teacher or principal once she gets to school"*

Dealing with intimidation is a classic situation faced by children—and parents—in every community. Our children struggle with being called names, being picked on, being excluded, not knowing how to make friends, or being the ones acting unkindly or aggressively toward others. It starts early and it can be devastating.

Luckily, normal development and childhood play can also present opportunities to teach our children how to get along, how to be considerate of everyone, and how to deal with conflict and develop resilience. But these skills don't come naturally to most kids. We really have to get in there and teach them how to behave—literally what to say and do. As soon as they are old enough to interact with others, children can learn not to be bullies and not to be targets. Our job as parents is to give them words to express their feelings, skills to monitor and change their behaviors, and conflict resolution strategies from the earliest age.

Ask your child what bullying is or who the bullies at school are. By kindergarten, most kids can tell you exactly who they are and what they do. If your child doesn't know, a simple definition is: a bully is someone who hurts someone else on purpose.

Bullying is a form of abuse—and as this chapter will show, it takes many forms. While psychologists often call it *peer abuse* or *peer-to-peer abuse,* I will refer to those children who are unkind and aggressive to others as *bullies* and those children who are the recipients of bullying as *targets.* I am very specific about not referring to targeted children as *victims* because I do not want "victim" to be a part of any targeted child's self-concept. Labeling a child a victim can put him or her on the road to self-defeating behaviors that perpetuate that label. *Bystanders* are all the children who are neither bullies nor targets. These are the kids who see what is happening but do nothing, usually because they don't know what to do or because they are afraid the bully will turn on them.

DID YOU KNOW?

- Conservative estimates by Norwegian researcher Dan Olweus are that 15 percent of students are bullied regularly.
- Recent studies in the U.S. have found that up to 80 percent of middle-school children admit to experiencing bullying behavior, including physical aggression, social ridicule, teasing, name-calling, and threats, at least once a month.
- Bullies and targets are often the same people, bullied one day and bullying the next. Numerous studies, including one from the University of Illinois, have found that "kids who bully a lot have been targeted, too."

What Is Bullying Behavior?

Bullying is the deliberate and repeated infliction of harm on another person. It takes many forms: physical, emotional, and verbal, or a combination of these. It may involve one child bullying another, a group of children against a single child, or one group against another group. It is not unlike other forms of abuse in that it involves the following:

- An imbalance of power.
- Differing emotional tones (the target of the bullying will be upset, whereas the bully is usually cool and in control)
- Bullies blaming the target for what has happened, and the target often thinking he or she somehow caused the bullying and accepting the accompanying guilt

- Lack of compassion or concern on the part of the bully for the targeted person
- A cycle that will continue—and escalate—without intervention

Bullying is typically associated with the more physically aggressive behaviors preferred by boys, but bullying includes many more subtle, and equally hurtful, behaviors that are perpetrated by boys and girls pretty equally. Targets of bullying are also as likely to be girls as boys, and bullying by groups of children is widespread.

Physical bullying includes hitting, pushing, kicking, pinching, spitting, tripping, and physical violence. Other examples are locking another child into a small space, putting a child's head in the toilet, giving wedgies or pulling someone's pants down, or inflicting unwanted sexual contact. As boys become older and stronger, physical bullying becomes more aggressive and violent. In adolescence there is an increase in sexual harassment as a form of bullying.

Verbal Bullying

Verbal bullying is typically thought of as name-calling, teasing, mimicking, taunting, shouting, cursing, and belittling. This can range from "fatso" to "klutz" to "retard." As children become older, bullying may include hateful speech, including gay bashing, racial or ethnic supremacist comments, and slurs regarding physical or mental differences. Verbal bullying intensifies in middle and high school and can be brutal, affecting the self-confidence and self-esteem of the strongest kids. The power of peers is most visible in this arena.

Relational Bullying

Relational bullying includes shunning, gossip, exclusion, starting rumors, abusive peer pressure, taunting, pranks, and setting the target up for an embarrassing or dangerous situation. Comments and pranks that are "just a joke" are often part of this form of bullying, and make it easy for bystander kids to get more involved in isolating the target.

Jokes that occur at the expense of another child are really a reflection of the bully's lack of empathy or compassion. The same can be said of bystanders who observe, accept, or encourage jokes and slurs. While they may start out doing nothing because they are afraid that they will themselves become a target, they quickly become desensitized and disengaged from the individuality and humanity of the person being bullied. At that point, they encourage or, by their silence or inaction, allow the bullying to continue.

This form of bullying is especially hard for targeted children to communicate and for adults to appreciate because it can be very subtle. In fact, parents and teachers sometimes take the side of the bully, thinking that a "good kid" wouldn't behave this way. Once the groundwork has been laid, a relational bully can completely debilitate his or her target with the smallest act: a look, a stare, or a small mutually understood motion. For example, think of the second- or third-grade girl who puts her hand to her mouth and whispers to another girl while looking right at her target. The imagination of a bullied child takes over from there.

Cyber-bullying

Cyber-bullying is the latest addition to the bully's arsenal. Examples are any abuse that is perpetrated electronically, such as text messages, voice mail, e-mail, Web sites, videotape, and instant messaging. This form of abuse allows multiple perpetrators and multiple voyeurs. For example, a girl might take an embarrassing picture of another girl in the dressing room and then send it to all of her friends. This sets up a situation where they are viewing the picture and passing it on, while the targeted child may not know for days what has happened. Cyber-bullying is vicious, hard to ignore, and capable of building its own momentum as the perpetrators get increasing attention from their audience. As a parent, you really need to pay attention to this one. Most of us are not on the same electronic trajectory as our kids, and it takes some focus to keep up. In Day 9, I will discuss this fully.

PHYSICAL	VERBAL	RELATIONAL	CYBER-BULLYING
Hitting	Name-calling	Peer pressure	Rumors
Pushing	Teasing	Exclusion	Gossip
Kicking	Being mean	Gossip	E-mails
Shoving	Making fun	Threatening	Voice mails
Pinching	Bad language	Setting up to get in trouble	Web postings
Violence	Verbal abuse	Belittling	Text messaging
Abusive behavior	Bossiness	Ganging up on someone	Pictures
Destructive behavior	Shouting	Name-calling	Impersonation
Spitting	Taunting	Pranks	Harassment
Tripping	Cursing	Harassment	Threats

Who Are the Bullies?

Q: *"The day my son was suspended for bullying was one of the most shocking days of my life. My son was always quiet and well-behaved. He didn't make trouble or get in people's faces. What he did do was drop open cans of Coke into other kids' backpacks, squeeze toothpaste into their lockers, and drop gummy worms into their snow boots. He didn't fit my picture of a bully. As we began to talk about the problem, I learned that he had been bullied for years. Instead of telling us, he had found a way to bully back."*

—Molly K., *parent of nine-year-old*

SHERRYLL SAYS: *"This is so often the case. Kids who are bullied soon learn that they can bully someone else who is younger or smaller. Parents often find out that their child has been a target of bullying at the same time they learn that they need to address their child's being a bully. Intervention for your son should include stopping the bullying behavior by setting clear behavioral expectations and consequences. At the same time, it is important to talk about the anger and sense of powerlessness he experienced when he was the target of another bully. This combination will increase his empathy for others, give him better social skills, and improve his ability to make friends."*

A Bully Can Be Anyone

Some children become bullies because they lack insight and respect for others. Often, former targets turn into bullies as soon as they are big enough, strong enough, or clever enough to bully someone else. Sometimes bullies are children experiencing life situations they can't cope with, that leave them feeling helpless and out of control. They may be children with poor social skills, who do not fit in, who can't meet the expectations of their family or school. They may bully others to feel competent, to control someone else, or to ease their own feelings of powerlessness. Some children take part in group bullying because it gives them a feeling of safety—assurance that they won't become the target—and a connection with power that they don't have on their own. Bullies' behavior often intensifies over time as the response to their aggression is reinforced by the reactions of people around them, including the targets of their bullying.

TALK WITH YOUR KIDS

What children see on television and in movies shapes their view of how the world works. It is worth discussing what your children think about what they are watching. Questions to ask might include:

- Can you think of any cartoon characters that are bullies?
- Do people think it's funny? Do you think it's funny?
- Would it be funny in real life? Why? Why not?

Characteristics of Bullies

Psychology research is consistent about the characteristics of bullies. Following are some of the traits that may appear in any number of combinations:

- May have been a target of physical or emotional abuse and bullying at the hands of others
- Is angry, revengeful, and focused on angry thoughts
- Tends to have little empathy for others
- Has poor understanding of social cues and cultural norms

- Is quick to anger and responds with force
- Sees aggression as a way to preserve self-image
- Inappropriately perceives hostile intent in the actions of others
- Has learned to control others through verbal threats and physical actions
- Chronically repeats aggressive behaviors
- Experiences a feeling of power and control from bullying

In the classroom and in the community, bullies show up in different forms. There is the swaggering, confident bully, usually a boy, who is often blatant about his bullying and proud of his ability to control others. He tends to be more physical, and people get out of his way when he approaches. This bully steals lunches, pushes kids around, is often verbally aggressive, and is the most likely to be identified because his behavior is so clear. There is also the type of bully who is socially awkward and easily provoked, who often goads kids into responding to him. These kids often do not understand why other people do not want to be around them, and they become more aggressive in their attempts to belong.

Girls are usually the social bullies, controlling the social scene with gossip, rumors, shunning, and cyber-bullying. They build power groups by making fun of and excluding others. This group is often hard to identify and even harder to change. They enjoy their social power and are often high achievers, well liked by adults. Then there are the groups of boys or girls who use the power of their social group to victimize others. This may include anything from gangs to groups of young people associated with sports, school clubs, or socio-economic groups. These kids are also often good students who are well liked by their peers and by adults.

DID YOU KNOW?

Being a bully has a long-term impact on young people. There appears to be a significant relationship between bullying others and experiencing later legal and criminal problems as an adult.

- In one study, 60 percent of those characterized as bullies in grades six through nine had at least one criminal conviction by age twenty-four.

- Chronic bullies seem to maintain their behaviors into adulthood, negatively influencing their ability to develop and maintain positive relationships.

Early Intervention Matters

Bullying is learned behavior, and, without intervention, bullies continue to bully. This is one reason it is important to be aware of children who are more aggressive as preschoolers, as they are likely to carry this behavior into their school years. Preschool is the age when patterns are established or redirected most effectively. In *The Schoolyard Bully,* Kim Zarzour identifies several key warning signs to help spot an excessively aggressive preschooler. While any one of these may occur occasionally, a pattern of these behaviors is a warning sign not only in preschool but into kindergarten and early elementary school:

1. Intentionally breaks toys
2. Provokes or annoys other people on purpose
3. Displays a lack of empathy or conscience
4. Hurts animals
5. Hurts others, throws objects when upset

A parent's response to these behaviors is very important. It sets the tone for expectations and acceptable ways to behave. For example, I was in a Halloween store recently and observed an interchange that modeled a parent dealing with this behavior effectively. While walking down the mask aisle, a younger preschool boy started to cry and cling to his mother. An older preschool boy started to laugh at him and called him a scaredy cat. The older boy's mother said, "That's not very nice of you. You should be trying to let him know it's only make believe, not make him feel worse." The older boy then apologized and took the younger boy's hand and showed him that the masks weren't scary at all once you had them in your hand.

Another important pattern that requires steadfast intervention is the young child who provokes others on purpose, displays a lack of concern for others, hurts others, or displays destructive or aggressive behavior when upset. Believing that your child will outgrow these behaviors or develop greater sensitivity later on is a mistake. These young children need concrete feedback and consequences:

- "It is not all right to bother (annoy, upset, disturb, irritate) other people just because you are bored (upset, irritated, annoyed, jealous)."
- "You may not treat other people (siblings, friends, toys, pets) that way. Let's think about a better way to say that you are upset (angry, jealous, sad)."
- "After you spend five minutes in time-out, we will talk about a better way to get your sister's attention (share your friend's toys, play with the dog, let me know you are angry)."

If you have a child who struggles with these behaviors, address it now. Communicate clearly the consequences of aggressive behavior, and impose them consistently. Follow up with role-play and modeling of acceptable behaviors, so your child is not only absolutely clear about your expectation, but also experiences his ability to be successful. Remember that this can be an uncomfortable process for adults who feel shy or unsure or are still developing better assertiveness skills themselves. It is perfectly all right to be building your own life skills as you work with your child.

INTERVENTIONS FOR AGGRESSIVE CHILDREN

1. State your expectations and your values clearly and often. *We treat other people with kindness. We are not mean to people. We do not hurt others. We do not take things that don't belong to us.*

2. Establish boundaries and rules for appropriate behavior, and talk about them when your child is not upset. Then be vigilant about using praise when your child is kind or considerate, meets the behavioral expectations you have set, or solves a conflict calmly and appropriately. Be clear about what your child has done well. "You told her exactly how you felt without yelling. That is a wonderful way to solve problems."

3. Respond to aggression with clear messages. "Throwing things is not all right. If you are angry, please use your words and tell me what is wrong." Role-play and model ways to communicate feelings without hurting others.

4. Establish consequences for failing to act within these boundaries and rules. It is critical that consequences not be physical. Spanking or other forms of aggres-

sive consequences give the wrong message and only make things worse for the aggressive child. Use logical consequences, time-outs, and withdrawal of privileges in response to aggressive behavior.

5. Be aware that societal messages may not support what you are trying to do. Be alert to social messages, limit television to nonaggressive shows, avoid video games that are aggressive or competitive, and keep reality shows and television news out of sight.

Who Are the Targets of Bullying?

Q: *"My son is quite small for his age and wears glasses. He is very smart, reads already, and loves to talk about dinosaurs, archaeology, and his rock collection. He has come home on several days with his model dinosaurs and rocks broken. He didn't want to tell me what had happened, but I badgered him until he did. Apparently, he is being victimized by some older boys who act as if they are interested and then break his things and give them back to him, pretending to be 'really sorry.' We want him to learn to handle situations like this for himself, but we're not sure how to go about it."*

—Mary A., *parent of six-year-old*

SHERRYLL SAYS: *"It is easy for kids to be picked on when their enthusiasm for something sets them apart. At this age, I would say the real problem is lack of supervision at the school. I would recommend two approaches. First, I think it is appropriate to let the school know what is going on so they can increase supervision. First graders should not be left without supervision. Second, I would work with your son on strategies that will allow him to share his interests with*

less risk. You might role-play showing an interest in his dinosaurs,
asking to hold them. He can practice saying, 'I'd rather you just
looked at them without touching them. They are pretty fragile.'
As he gets older, he will become more adept at identifying those
children who really share his interests."

Anyone Can Be a Target of Bullying.

Although no one is immune, the personal skills children have
may affect the length and severity of bullying. Children who seem
less able to fend off bullies often have poorer social skills, lower
self-esteem, and a small or nonexistent support group. Other
children learn to be targets, preferring negative attention to no
attention at all. These children may make themselves targets by
teasing bullies, egging them on, and then not knowing what to
do when the bully turns on them.

According to research to date, children who are targeted over
extended periods of time tend to show one or more of the following characteristics:

- Introverted, cautious, anxious, sensitive, or unassertive
- Few friends or hang on the fringe
- Physically weaker, smaller, or physically different
- Socially immature
- Likely to react to bullying with withdrawal or tears
- Rarely tell or make a fuss about what has happened
- Low self-concept, including feeling stupid, unattractive, or
  unsuccessful

However, because children who are targeted for bullying haven't
received nearly the level of research attention garnered by bullies,
it's likely that the kids described above are only part of the population of kids whose lives are shaped by bullying. When I listen
to kids, especially adolescents, discuss bullying, it is clear that

anyone who looks or acts different—including strong kids trying to do the right thing, high-achieving students, artists and other creative types—can be targeted by the mainstream population simply because they do not fit the "norm."

Learning how to get along in a variety of social situations, learning to go with the social flow, learning to be yourself even if you are outside the mainstream, and learning strong conflict-resolution skills are lifelong processes that you'll help foster in your children in the following days of this ten-day program.

DID YOU KNOW?

- Children who are bullied are often anxious, insecure, and cautious.
- They may suffer from low self-esteem and rarely defend themselves.
- They may retaliate when confronted by students who bully them.
- They are often socially isolated and lack social skills.
- One study found that the most frequent reason cited by youth for persons being bullied is that they "didn't fit in."
- Males who are bullied tend to be physically weaker than their peers.

Why Targeted Children Don't Tell

Children learn about social interaction in the preschool and early elementary-school years. They learn that hitting, pinching, and biting are not permitted. They learn that lesser levels of conflict, such as taking another child's toys, interrupting, harsh words, and small physical conflicts are something "kids need to learn to work out among themselves." They learn not to be tattletales. They learn that it's not all right to run to a grownup every time they have a problem they don't know how to solve. They're told to "toughen up."

In other words, they learn very early on that there is an imbalance of power and control among children that they should know how to handle. But most young children have never been taught what to do in response. They think that they missed something along the way, that they should know how to handle these situations, or that they should be more thick-skinned. They may not ask for help because they feel guilty, helpless, or afraid they will be ridiculed.

Older children fail to report bullying for some of the same reasons, but older children have the added fear that telling or asking for help will only make the bullying escalate. They have experienced adults who don't handle bullying very well, who are often glib in their advice to "ignore it," or "just avoid the bully," or not to be "so sensitive." In fact, many children perceive that adults condone the bullying behavior and support the bully over the targeted child. Older children may have also found that the bully maintains the upper hand even with adult intervention. After reporting the problem, the targeted child may be even more terrorized in the bathroom, in the hallway, or after school, when adults are not present. This is a result of poor management of bullying issues by adults and will only change when adults understand more clearly the dynamics of bullying so they can respond without placing the focus directly back on the target.

One of the most upsetting and confusing things about bullying is the length of time it takes targeted children to speak up. Many children experience bullying for years before it is discovered. Some never tell at all. I often meet adults who only recognize that what they experienced was bullying when they hear me describe the many ways in which children can be targeted. For example, those who experienced rumors and gossip and isolation during high school may have been profoundly unhappy without ever realizing that they were being bullied.

Why don't kids tell?

1. Most kids don't tell because they are taught not to "tattle." In order to combat this problem, make the distinction with your kids between reporting a problem and tattling. *Tattling* means telling on someone just so you can get them in trouble. *Telling someone that you need help (or that someone you know needs help) is not tattling—it is smart and responsible.*

2. The second reason kids don't tell is that they learn very early on that adults expect them to deal with interpersonal conflict on their own. Many times I have heard parents and teachers walk away after a kid has asked for help, saying, "You two need to work it out." But if kids knew how, they would have done so already! The proper response to a request for help is to model and practice how to "work it out"!

3. Kids who are bullied may also mistakenly think the bullying is their fault, that they did something wrong or somehow deserve what has happened to them. This is not surprising; kids are ego-centered. They think they cause most of what happens in their young worlds. As children get older, embarrassment becomes a key reason they don't reveal what is happening to them. They think they ought to be able to handle whatever situations they find themselves in, and they don't want to ask for help and admit their vulnerability.

4. Finally, targeted kids often don't tell because the adults seem to be on the bully's side. Think about kids from your middle-school or hight-school days who had real social power—for example, athletes, cheerleaders, school newspaper staff, and other students who brought accolades to the school. Chances are, you remember

them being supported by parents, school personnel, community members, and peers.

Whether they win National Merit Scholarships or athletic championship trophies, kids who bring glory to the school, who make the school or community look good, are given social power. Some of these students use their power to bully others—directly, by pushing their weight around, and indirectly, by exclusion or gossip. Imagine being a target of someone this powerful and trying to bring it to the attention of adults who seem to adore the bully. Asking for help can feel demeaning, frightening, and overwhelming. One of your key tasks is to give children the clear and consistent message that they should tell you if they are being mistreated, and that you will believe them and help them. Giving your kids permission to talk about anything and everything, even if it is dumb or embarrassing or hard to believe, can go a long way toward stopping bullying behaviors. But this is not a one-time message; it is something that you need to tell your children in many different ways as they get older.

TALK WITH YOUR KIDS

- If you got accused of doing something at school that you didn't do, would you tell me about it?
- Do you think I would believe you?
- If you did something to a friend that wasn't very nice and wanted to apologize, what would you say?
- If you couldn't figure it out, would you ask for help?
- Whom would you ask?

Eight Myths about Bullying

There is no shortage of myths about bullying. Among the most common mis-perceptions:

Myth 1: **Bullying is a boys' issue.**
Reality: Boys and girls are bullies equally. Bullying by males tends to be more overt and physical. Bullying by girls tends to be more emotionally based and harder to spot, such as exclusion, gossip, and rumors.

Myth 2: **Bullies are just looking for attention.**
Reality: Bullying is about power and control. It is more often than not a hidden activity, seen only by the bully's circle of friends and targets.

Myth 3: **Bullying is just a normal part of growing up.**
Reality: Bullying is abusive and damaging to everyone involved. It is a learned behavior that has been tolerated rather than corrected and eliminated.

Myth 4: **Most bullying occurs outside of school.**
Reality: Where children congregate is where bullying occurs. Schools are full of bullies of all kinds.

Myth 5: **Cliques are a natural part of growing up.**
Reality: Cliques are exclusionary by definition and exist in a culture of judging others. This is different from friendships, which are fluid and inclusive.

Myth 6: **Targets of bullying should "toughen up."**
Reality: This is like telling a victim of domestic violence or sexual abuse to toughen up. Bullying is interpersonal violence, and the target of it should not be expected to change to accommodate the bullying.

Myth 7: **Telling an adult won't change a thing.**
Reality: While many children have experienced this, adults need to learn to intervene more effectively, and

children need to learn to tell, and keep telling, until someone helps.

Myth 8: **Targets ask for it.**
Reality: No one wants to be bullied. While it may appear that some children with poor social skills are aggravating a bully, the bottom line is that there is no excuse for bullying.

Myths usually hold elements of truth and may represent the experience of some people, but bullying really encompasses all groups, places, and times. It is damaging to bullies, to their targets, and to the communities in which they live and attend school. It is true that adults often don't understand or intervene. But, in my experience, adults will take action if we give them more tools, and if we teach kids to keep asking for help until they get it!

The message to relay to your kids from the earliest possible age is that *everyone* deserves and has a right to be treated with respect. When we excuse bullying as something that boys do naturally, as playing around, or as something that toughens you up or is a normal part of growing up, we give the wrong message. When we teach children "sticks and stones may break your bones but words will never hurt you," we may inadvertently diminish the sting of bullying and, in essence, excuse the behavior of bullies. As Robert Fulghum, author of *All I Really Need to Know I Learned in Kindergarten,* so accurately says, "Sticks and stones can break my bones, but words can break my heart."

Therefore, even when kids as young as preschool age begin to call people names or use unkind words, we have a responsibility to intervene immediately and consistently. By first grade, children learn the power of exclusion. We begin to hear things like: "She's not my friend and she can't come to my party." In the early elementary grades, little groups develop that can be quite exclusionary and cruel. By the later elementary grades and into middle school, cliques become increasingly powerful by means of gossip, rumors, and exclusion. Technology has become a major venue for this cruel behavior.

All forms of bullying need to be identified in their earliest stages. As you embark on this program with your kids, the message needs to be crystal clear: bullying is mean spirited, inconsiderate, and hurtful behavior and is completely unacceptable.

TALK WITH YOUR KIDS

- If your child points at someone on the street, ask, "How do you think that person feels when you point at him?"
- If there is a new kid in your child's school who dresses differently or who speaks another language, ask, "How do you think she feels? How could you include her and make her feel more at home?"
- If you learn that other kids are picking on a child, ask, "What could you do to let the other kids know it's not all right to treat her this way?"

Be Aware of Adult Bullying Behaviors

It is important for each of us to look carefully at the tone of our speaking and our actions. Are there ways in which we celebrate interpersonal violence or engage in bullying ourselves? Do we say things like "She had that coming!" or "What did he think was going to happen when he said that?" Do we encourage our kids to "tell it like it is" or "let him have it"? Are we rude or condescending when service is not to our liking, or abusive when someone else gets to the gas pump at the same moment we do? Do we honk or yell at other drivers on the road?

We need to look at the messages we give children in our own relationships. Do we gossip or say unkind things about other people in front of our children? Do we express anger or hostility toward a classroom teacher after a meeting? How do we interact with other parents and children at gymnastics, Little League, or Peewee Football? While anger is a natural part of life, children don't always understand the full range of the feelings we have or the details of the situation. All they see is our behavior, which may look a lot like bullying and may very well appear frightening and violent.

Children easily recognize who the bullies are in their environment because the "scripts" of bullying are ever-present, from cartoons to television to conversations among adults. Think of the number of television shows that are built around getting a laugh at someone else's expense. It's easy for kids to learn that making fun of others gives them power, influence, or attention, all of which can be heady feelings and a powerful reward for the child's behavior.

Laughter is another of these incredibly powerful social rewards. This is one of the reasons children are sometimes willing to be the butt of jokes. They decide early on that they would rather showcase their deficits or differences than be bullied for them. It's how children learn that showing off, clowning around, and making themselves look foolish are worth the negative consequences. They know that perceived weakness makes them fodder for bullies, so they throw themselves in front of the train by joking or making a fool of themselves, rather than be pushed by a bully.

This social learning about the power of an audience and the mixed messages children get from the media and the adults in their lives are central to the problem of bullying. By understanding and observing these social messages, we derive many of the tools to stop this pattern of behavior.

DAY 1: SUMMING IT UP

Bullying is a social phenomenon that has been accepted to a large degree. But bullying is not a normal part of growing up; it is another form of child abuse.

Children aren't born bullies; they learn to be bullies. Some things to watch for in your child include:

- Quick to anger
- Tries to control others physically or with threats
- Repeats aggressive behaviors
- Perceives hostile intent on the part of others
- Focuses on angry and vengeful thoughts
- Sees aggression as a way to preserve self-image
- Gets feelings of power and control from bullying
- Has been a target of bullying in the past

Children who are targeted for bullying also share some common characteristics. If you see these in your child, you can actively work to develop life skills that will reduce his or her vulnerability. Pay attention if your child:

- Has few friends or prefers to hang on the sidelines
- Is physically smaller or weaker or has physical differences
- Is very cautious, anxious, sensitive, or unassertive
- Has feelings hurt easily or cries easily

- Has a low self-concept, including feeling stupid or different

Bullying includes many behaviors, including:

- Physical: Hitting, pushing, kicking, pinching, spitting, tripping, physical violence, making faces, grimacing, and hand gestures
- Verbal: Name-calling, teasing, mimicking, taunting, shouting, cursing, and hate speech
- Relational: Gossip, exclusion, rumors, peer pressure, pranks, and harassment

Taking Action: If Your Child Is Being Bullied or Is a Bully

Q: *"My child has been bullied for almost a year. The boys in his class throw things at him, take his hat, hide his lunch, and push him when the teachers aren't looking. He has come home crying so many times, it breaks my heart. There are two teacher aides who are supposed to watch the kids at recess, which is when most of the bullying happens, but they seem not to care. My son is very sensitive, shy, and doesn't seem to change his behavior even though we've talked about this many times."*

—Tammy S., *parent of six-year-old*

SHERRYLL SAYS: *"Your son is caught in the gap between concepts and skills. Talking about what he needs to do doesn't give him the skills he needs to stand up to this bullying. Because he is shy and not very assertive he needs role-play in order to build his skills. He needs lots of practice in speaking up and using body language that communicates to the bullies that enough is enough. In addition, supervision is the responsibility of the school. Request a meeting to discuss the problem and the need to increase supervision. You might also want to initiate a discussion about the school's response to bullying, how all students can learn what bullying is, and how the school can work with students to stop it."*

If you've skipped straight to this chapter, you know how painful it is to see your child being bullied, and you probably feel helpless. Today I'll walk you step-by-step through the actions you and your child can take to stop existing bullying and prevent future bullying. Keep in mind that this may take some time as your child builds his confidence, learns the skills in the following chapters, and develops a support system for himself.

Bullies are not sensitive, empathetic types who will respond to your child's plea for fairness or reasonableness, or to statements about how the bullying is making your child feel. Bullies are trying to cause distress. They want your child to be upset, afraid, and intimidated. They crave power and control, and will continue their bullying until they get bored or are stopped.

Bullies are aggressive and look for opportunities to intimidate, by catching a child in the bathroom, in the corner of the locker room, or while walking home. And bullies smell fear from a child who sees them and walks the other way. They find more ways to taunt, tease, and intimidate the child who hangs his head and hurriedly walks to class.

Therefore, the best way to stop existing bullying is for your child to learn that bullying is not his fault, that it is not something he has to put up with, that there are actions he can take to stop the bullying, and that he can expect adults to help as well.

Signs That Your Child May Be a Target of Bullying

When children change, when they become more quiet or withdrawn or aggressive, we need to learn to ask questions. Children think that we know what is going on for them, that we can somehow read their minds or their faces. We need to tell them that this is not so. When they have a problem, they need to tell us, to ask for help. But too often they don't, so there are some signs that can alert you to ask questions. Pay attention if your child:

- Stops playing outside after school
- Often feels a little bit too sick to go to school
- Asks to be picked up rather than walking home from school
- Loses interest in past friends
- Doesn't want to talk about what is happening at school
- Begins to do poorly in school
- Has torn clothing or comes home looking scuffed up

Any of these could be a sign of bullying. Some children try to tell in indirect ways (see Anne's story, below). If you have a concern, ask questions. Tell your child that it is safe to talk with you about a problem at school, that you won't do anything to make it worse. Make reference to the mistaken beliefs that keep kids from asking for help:

- I can handle it myself.
- I will just ignore it and it will stop.
- It's probably my fault that this is happening.
- I don't want to seem soft or immature.

All of these mistaken beliefs can keep a child from telling.

Asking the Right Questions

Q: *"We moved to this country earlier this year. About a month into the school year, my daughter, Analise, began coming home after school and taking a bath. She would sometimes take another bath right before bed and then again before she went to school. At first I thought maybe she was being sexually abused and tried to talk to her about it. After a few days, she told me that the kids at school were taunting her, telling her that her skin was dirty because her skin color is darker than theirs. How can I possibly address this?"*

—Anna M., *mother of six-year-old*

SHERRYLL SAYS: *"Children are not naturally accepting of individual differences. They need to learn about individual differences and cultural differences. I would go to your child's teacher and school principal and explain what has happened. You might want to offer to put together a classroom day of awareness about your country and heritage. Your child's teacher should watch for opportunities to talk about how our behaviors make other people feel, and plan activities to teach acceptance and celebration of individual differences. What your child needs to hear from you is an acknowledgement of the cruelty and ignorance of her peers and how hurtful it is to hear their comments even if she knows they are not true. Try coaching her on some responses such as, 'I'm from South America, our skin is naturally darker than yours.' As she learns to address their insults in a straightforward way, their ability to impact her emotionally will diminish."*

If handling bullying were easy, it wouldn't be the problem that it is. As a parent, you may find it difficult to work with your child to address the problem, when your instinct will be to storm into the school and to rail at the bully's parents in order to protect your child. But once the bullying is out in the open, I've found that children are pretty good at telling us what they need from us, if we listen to them. As you and your child work to resolve the bullying problem, keep the discussion alive so you have opportunities to congratulate your child for successes and to regroup if s/he needs to try another strategy.

Always remember that children are directly affected by their perception of their well-being in their environment. If we talk to them in a way that makes them feel more fearful or insecure, we heighten their sense of vulnerability. Children who are frightened have fewer options and less self-confidence to handle life events effectively. My goal in this book is to help you talk to your children in a way that makes them feel confident, capable, and informed, so they can actually be more effective in protecting themselves.

DID YOU KNOW?

- Bullying takes on different forms in boys and girls.
- Both boys and girls say that others bully them by making fun of the way they look or talk, but boys are more likely to report being hit, slapped, or pushed.
- Girls are more likely than boys to report being the targets of rumors and sexual comments.
- While boys target both boys and girls, girls most often bully other girls, using more subtle and indirect forms of aggression than boys.

If your child tells you about a bullying situation, or you suspect one, ask questions that draw out details. For example, you might say, "I noticed that you don't want to walk home from school anymore. Can you tell me what is happening that you don't like?" Or, "Did something happen between you and Amanda that you don't want to see her anymore?"

As you learn more, be calm and hold your tongue. Don't jump in with judgmental statements, such as, "Maybe if you were a little nicer, she would be nicer." Be accepting of what you are hearing, and ask questions that fill in the blanks. Likewise, don't minimize the bullying or make excuses for the bully with offhand comments such as, "Oh, don't let it bother you," "She's probably not very good at making friends," or "Try to be friendlier to her." Bullying is incredibly painful, and your child wants you to validate how she is feeling, not to side with the bully.

Kids know that bullying is a problem that simplistic catchphrases will not address. The advice kids get is usually limited to:

- Ignore the bully.
- Just walk away.
- Stay with a friend.

While each of these suggests a more comprehensive strategy that may work (and I'll talk more about these specific tools on Day 7), throwaway advice like this says to kids that we aren't taking their concerns seriously, that we don't understand what is really going on, and that we aren't a very good resource to help them solve the problem. So while my advice for kids who are being bullied includes building as many of these prevention skills as they can, there are other immediate steps to be taken.

Really listen to what your child's words and demeanor are saying. Is your child afraid, intimidated, confused, hopeless, sad, angry, or vindictive? Be calm and thoughtful. Respond rather than react. Your child is paying very close attention to your response and making a decision about whether or not to talk with you about this anymore. Be supportive of how your child is feeling. For example, what if your child tells you that he is "going to take a bat and knock the bully out"? A proper response might be, "I can hear how angry you are about the way he treated you, and that you want to hurt him back. Maybe we could talk about some other ways to deal with this problem."

If your child is feeling hopeless about the situation, you might respond by saying, "I can see that you've tried a lot of ways to solve this problem by yourself, and you think it will never stop."

It is important to acknowledge that this is a difficult and complex problem and that you know there may not be any simple or easy answers. The older your child is, the more likely this is to be true.

After you've had some time to think and perhaps read some of the ideas in this book, come back to the conversation and ask your child what strategies he or she has already tried in response to the bullying. Ask questions like, "What else have you tried?" "Why do you think that didn't work?" or, "What did your teacher say when you told her?"

Kids need to know that you are there to help and that you want to know what's going on. You can help problem-solve, but don't assume your child wants you to jump in and do something. Many children are afraid that things will only get worse if parents talk to the school or to the bully's parents. And often they are right. Until you are sure that your child has tried everything s/he can, or there is an imminent physical threat, give your child the opportunity to address the problem without your intervention.

Your Anti-Bullying Action Plan

While the following chapters will help you build specific skills, there are a few elements that carry throughout. As you role-play with your child, you will want to develop your child's ability to project confidence, to manage doubts and anxiety, and to utilize role-play to build strategies and skills.

Step 1: Build Your Child's Confidence: "Fake it till you make it."

Being immune to the tactics of bullies begins with projecting confidence and self-assuredness. For example, children who keep their head down, shoulders hunched forward, hands in pockets, and who look from side to side watching for anyone who shows up, are more likely to be picked on. On the other hand, children who stand up tall, head up and eyes forward, arms by their sides, walking with assurance, will actually begin to feel more confident.

What is interesting is that we can change how children feel by changing how they present themselves. We tend to believe that how we act is a function of how we feel. However, there is ample evidence that the opposite is true—that how a child acts directly influences how s/he feels. A common phrase, "Fake it till you make it," reflects that. So working with a child to stand up tall, to look you in the eye, and to speak in a clear and firm voice actually builds self-confidence. Then, when people are more responsive, the behavior is reinforced, and the child is more likely to continue the confident stance.

This is part of what you want to accomplish in the role-play. You want to give your child the experience of being more confident and accomplished and powerful. You should feel free to adapt the role-plays in this book to build your child's confidence, so that he or she can actually be seen as someone who is not going to be bullied.

Step 2: Deal with Anxiety and Fear Directly

Your child's demeanor broadcasts volumes. If you have a child who is fearful or anxious, it is worthwhile to name those feelings, to identify where your child feels the anxiety or nervousness (in the legs, stomach, or chest). Discuss openly what it feels like, what thoughts accompany the feelings, and how to counteract those thoughts and feelings—breathing being the best and most universal technique.

Anxiety erodes confidence, and it shows. Pay attention to what your child's internal monologue is. If the internal message is "I'm not very good at . . ." "I can't do anything about this," or "I'm afraid he'll hurt me," it will be very hard to portray confidence. Changing your child's internal voice will help. After role-play, practice with your child saying positive statements aloud, to address a problem or frustration: "I am going to have a good morning." Or, "I'm a good problem-solver." If you have role-played a situation related to bullying, let your child know that you understand s/he may still feel a little anxious, but the self-talk should be: "I am not going to let this bully ruin my day. I can show him I am not afraid. I can project confidence. I will not put up with this for another day."

Step 3: Develop a Behavioral Plan and Role-Play

Whatever situations present themselves, play them out. Rehearse the situation until your child is assertive, clear, firm, and confident. Then change the situation slightly and practice again. You are building confidence and the ability to spontaneously respond to a variety of situations.

After any role-play, discuss how your child will communicate through body language that s/he is not vulnerable to or even interested in, for example, the past bullying behavior. Identify your child's strengths and the new skills s/he is learning, so that your child walks out the door feeling confident and armed with specific strategies to get through the challenges of the day.

Step 4: Role-Play Worst-Case Scenarios

Allow your child to discuss and role-play worst-case scenarios. Don't negate the fears. They will get in the way of your child's success if s/he isn't able to express them fully. Instead, role-play through the fears and continue to build confidence. For example, if you are working on a situation and your child continually comes back with, "What if this . . ?" and "What if that . . ?" do not be impatient. When a child does this, it is really a way of processing the many fears and anxieties s/he has about the situation. Working through them one at a time by role-playing helps relieve children's anxiety, builds their skills, and gives them the confidence to take on the problem.

Step 5: Debrief

Ask your child, "How did it go? What worked, what didn't?" "How should your strategy change?" "What is your plan for tomorrow?" Role-play and assist your child in refining the plan. For example, if your child was able to walk by the bully in the hall without acknowledging what the bully was saying, but still felt sick, you could have your child role-play walking by and, at the same time, thinking, "I will not let this bully get to me." Self-talk in the middle of a situation like this helps to take the child's mind off the fear and anxiety and builds confidence.

If your child is telling you that your suggestions really aren't helping, pay attention. Listen carefully to what your child has to say. We need to help children come up with strategies that they think will work for them. Sometimes having all the answers is another form of "rescuing." You want to be a cheerleader for your child finding his or her own solutions.

Step 6: Debrief Again

Keep track of how it's going without being irritating to your child. If things are not going well, brainstorm next steps with your child. "Do you need to get help from someone else?" "Is there a friend who can help?" "Do you need an adult's help?" Ask yourself if there are more long-term steps you want to take, such as getting your child involved in a self-defense class. Does the school know what is going on? If not, what is the best way to let them know? If they are aware of what is going on, how can you support your child without taking over?

There are times when adults need to intervene. If you determine that this is one of those times, do not hesitate, especially if your child is being threatened or is too afraid to go to school, or if there is any evidence of aggression or potential injury.

Should You Talk with Your Child's School— or the Bully's Parents?

It is preferable for children to advocate for themselves or ask for help from the adults in the school when they have a problem with bullying. You can help by role-playing with your child how to ask for help, how to tell the whole story, and how to respond to teacher suggestions. If your child is too young or is unsuccessful in resolving the situation, you may need to get involved. Approaching a bully's parents directly, once kids are of school age, rarely goes well. Contacting the school or community organization where the bullying is taking place is usually more successful.

When you approach the school, clearly and objectively describe the bullying behaviors without judgmental or pejorative words. You should listen carefully if they describe actions they have taken to date. This is easier said than done, because you will probably be feeling protective and anxious to ensure that something is done to protect your child. It is important to remember that most schools are not particularly skilled at dealing with bully problems, and they may not have much to offer.

If the school blames your child or says your child needs to toughen up, let them know that asking the target of bullying to change is not appropriate. Aggressive behavior needs to be dealt with, and you would like their assistance in doing so. If the school suggests a course of action that you support, ask them for a timeline so you know when to get back to them to follow up. Be aware that adult efforts to intervene often do little more than drive bullying further underground, so keep communications with your child and the school open, to ensure that you are not shut out because your child feels that your intervention only made matters worse.

Worst-Case Scenario: If Your Child Is in Danger and the School Is Not Responding

Many teachers, unfortunately, do not take bullying seriously enough. Parents contact me every day with truly unbelievable stories about schools and communities that refuse to respond. When this happens, when administrators are not responsive, an aggressive and documented approach to the problem is needed. The recommended steps include:

1. Log every contact with the school or community group.
2. Every contact should be followed up with a letter stating what happened, what action was taken, and what was promised. Parents should send a copy of this letter by certified mail, return receipt requested, to the person they met with, the principal, and—by the second or third meeting—to the superintendent of schools and members of the school board (or the organizational equivalent). It is not necessary to be threatening at this point; your form of communication should get their attention.
3. If your child is in danger or has been injured, call the police department and insist on filing a complaint, whether or not they want to take it or intend to do anything about it. If the problem involves an older child, call the Department of Social Services and make a child abuse report. If they do not want to take the report, ask to speak to a supervisor and again request that they take the report. If they still refuse, write to the department head documenting their refusal to take the report.
4. If the system continues not to respond, contact an attorney. Children have a right to be safe in their school and community.
5. If you feel your child is in danger and you feel you need to keep him out of school, let the school know in writing what you are doing and why. Send copies of this correspondence to

the school board and superintendent of schools. If you have reached this point, a lawyer is essential.

No parent ever wants to get to this step, but sometimes it has to be done. Be fearless in your advocacy for your child at this point, and remember that sometimes this is what it takes to create change for your child and others.

If Your Child Is a Bully

Q: *"My second grader's teacher has called me for the third time. She says my son is picking on other kids in the class until they cry. She says she has talked to him about it repeatedly, but he says he is 'just having a little fun.' I talked with him and he said the same thing. It's pretty clear to me that he likes the attention, he likes the power of being able to make the other kids cry, and he doesn't really care if his teacher puts him in time-out because he doesn't have to do his work while he's in time-out. Could this be a case of 'any attention is better than no attention at all'?"*

—Eve E., *mother of seven-year-old*

SHERRYLL SAYS: *"I think you hit the nail right on the head. He is getting lots of negative attention from the kids and from his teacher. You need to get together with his teacher and develop a behavioral plan that enables him to be rewarded for positive social interactions. The consequences of negative behavior should not include getting out of work. More appropriately, negative behaviors should result in his losing something he values—recess, perhaps, or free time later in the day. Ask the school to give you feedback on your son's behavior on a daily basis. What your child needs to hear from you is that his behavior is unacceptable to you, that you will be talking to his teacher daily, and that the consequences for his behavior will carry over at home. Quick intervention can absolutely turn this pattern around!"*

Relational bullying can be unbelievably cruel, and kids who participate in it often see it as "just the way things are." But it is no different from hitting someone with a stick. Children who are bullies need to be dealt with consistently and effectively. Bullying should not be overlooked or excused, no matter what the story.

DID YOU KNOW?

- It is a myth that bullies act tough in order to hide feelings of insecurity and self-loathing.
- Bullies tend to be quite confident, with high self-esteem.
- Bullies are typically physically aggressive, prone to violence, hot-tempered, easily angered, and impulsive, with a low tolerance for frustration.
- Bullies have a strong need to dominate others and little empathy for their targets.
- Male bullies are often physically bigger and stronger than their peers.
- Bullies tend to get in trouble more often, and to dislike and do poorly in school.

Bullying behavior increases as children get older, and the ramifications for bullies and the children around them are significant. At the same time, many bullies do not identify their behavior as bullying, and educating them is a critical part of changing their behavior.

1. The first step is to confront your child's behavior in a straightforward way, saying something like, "Your teacher called to tell

me that you have been on restricted lunch all week for bullying the younger children. What can you tell me about this?"

2. Do not blame or lecture. Listen first! A report that your child has been a bully is rarely the whole story, so give your child a chance to respond. Questions like, "Why would you do such a thing?" or "What were you thinking?" are not useful. The important question is "What happened?"

3. Once you have determined that your child acted like a bully or participated with others who were bullying, the key message is simple: bullying is unacceptable behavior—in your family and in society.

4. If what your child describes is bullying behavior, but your child doesn't recognize it as such, it is important to discuss the range of behaviors that constitute bullying (see Day 1). It is also important to help your child connect with how it feels to be treated that way. Empathy is the quality most often missing in children who do not see their behavior as bullying. I'll discuss this in more detail on Day 3.

5. Clearly lay out the consequences of the current incident as well as the consequences that will result if the aggression or bullying continues.

6. If your child is bullying in response to feeling frustrated, angry, or aggressive, discuss some alternatives to bullying. Bullies often lack basic social skills and need to understand and practice more appropriate ways to behave. As you teach the skills presented on Days 3, 5, 6, and 8, remember to act out the desired behaviors.

7. Be ready to listen when your child wants to talk about it. You want to stop the behavior, understand your child's feelings, and then teach and reward more appropriate behavior.

Bullying Begets Bullying

Q: *"I was cleaning my daughter's room and, as I went over the keys to her computer, I saw an e-mail she was writing that described her torment of another girl in her class. She described inviting the girl to meet her somewhere and then standing her up. She told about leaving anonymous notes in her backpack and making up rumors about her. My daughter was bragging about her mistreatment of this other girl. I was sick and confronted her as soon as she came home. Her response was 'Her friends did it to me, she deserves it back!'"*

—Cynthia T., *parent of middle-schooler*

SHERRYLL SAYS: *"This is so common in middle and high school. A culture of meanness develops as they bully each other back and forth, constantly looking for new ways to hurt each other. I recommend that you discuss with your daughter, and perhaps her friends, the possibility of declaring a cease-fire. Just as your daughter felt demeaned and angry about the way she was treated, her targets feel the same thing. Depending on the severity of the problem, it may be appropriate to approach the school and bring the problem to the attention of everyone at once, through classroom discussions and the creation of rules for electronic communications. If this fails, remind your daughter that all electronic communications are traceable, and harassment can be a crime."*

Remember that many children become bullies because they were targeted for bullying themselves. If there are prior bullying issues, it is always better to get help now than to have them come up again and again as your child grows. Consider whether your child needs professional help, such as anger management or other skill building, to address the issues that are causing the bullying behavior.

If your child bullies, ask how it feels to treat others in this way. Be aware that children sometimes like it. It may make them feel powerful and in control. (As I said earlier, bullies enjoy an audience and showing off for others.) Ask how s/he thinks the other person feels when treated this way. Most kids can recognize when they make another person feel bad. Make it clear to your child that this is aggressive behavior that is not acceptable precisely because it tramples the rights of someone else.

A discussion like this with a child who bullies is a powerful intervention, especially with preadolescent children. Often, they are not aggressive or bullying because they want to hurt someone else; rather, they don't have the skills to accomplish what they want. The bullying can then be an opportunity to teach alternate skills through discussion and role-play. Shifting from aggressive behavior to assertive behavior is discussed more fully on Day 6.

You should also talk with your child's school. Discuss with them what supports could be put in place so your child has more supervision and fewer chances to bully others. Determine consequences for bullying that you can support. Be certain that they know you want to be notified if there are additional problems. Listen if they have suggestions for addressing other problems that may be leading to the bullying behavior.

Stopping bullying while children are young truly shapes their future. Do not avert your eyes from this problem. It will only get worse, and the consequences will be more grave as your child gets older. In the next chapters, you will learn more about how to prevent bullying from getting worse and how to give a young bully the skills to interact with others more successfully.

DAY 2: SUMMING IT UP

It can be incredibly hard to hear that your child is a bully or is being bullied. But it is a call to action, because early intervention is the key.

If your child tells you he is being bullied:

- Listen, really listen to what he has to say about what is happening to him.
- Respond, don't react.
- Develop a strategy for responding to the bullying.
- Practice, practice, practice his possible responses. Remember that role-play is what takes the concepts and builds the skills he can really use.
- Debrief, regroup, and practice again.
- Acknowledge successes and continue to build skills.
- Get help if you need it!

If you learn that your child is the bully, it is equally important to listen and to act!

- Tell your child what you have heard.
- Do not blame or lecture—listen first.
- Ask questions.
- Set limits—this behavior is unacceptable.
- Set consequences, to teach taking responsibility for actions.
- Teach needed new skills.
- If necessary, get professional help.

Kids who are bullies, or who are targeted for bullying, need immediate and consistent help to change the patterns of interaction that lead to bullying and sustain it over time.

Developing Empathy for Others

Q: *"I am so embarrassed to admit that my son is a member of a group of boys who are harassing the special-needs kids in his classroom. They have made fun of them, pushed them around in the bathroom, stolen their school supplies, and called them names. My son is a nice kid and I cannot understand how he could do such a thing. When I confronted him, he admitted it but didn't seem to feel too bad about it. How can I help him be more empathetic?"*

—Jennifer M., *mother of middle-schooler*

SHERRYLL SAYS: *"First, be explicit with him that this is unkind and unacceptable behavior. The next step is helping him to figure out what he can do to make up for his cruel treatment of the special-needs kids. He might volunteer to teach them a sport or do a project with them. As he becomes more aware of them as people (rather than objectifying them as he has), he will be more empathetic. Third, ongoing discussion about individual differences and how our actions affect the feelings of others is important for your son. He needs to begin to see the world through eyes other than his own. Finally, teach him how to respond if his friends are behaving badly. If he witnesses unkind behavior, he needs to be willing and able to step forward and stop the bullying behavior by advocating for kind treatment of everyone."*

My favorite definition of self-esteem is "respect for self and esteem for others." Although this group of boys may have plenty of esteem for each other, they need to develop esteem for those outside their group. This may seem a simple concept, but helping kids put it into action each day takes effort, discipline, and commitment.

Helping Your Child Handle Emotions

We all have individual differences. For example, perhaps your child works fast and finds it incredibly annoying that other people work slowly. Or maybe your child gets irritated by other children in the classroom who are on the go all the time. It can be difficult for kids to negotiate the behaviors of others who don't do things "their way," and that's where teasing and social conflict start. Below are emotions that can lead to bullying behavior in childhood and into adulthood, if they are not balanced by the concept that everyone has a right to be heard, to be understood, and to be respected.

> **Reacting to hurt:** When someone makes fun of you, embarrasses you, or says something hurtful to you, your "fight or flight" presocialization instincts kick in. Your child may react by withdrawing or by wanting to give back more of the same. These are both natural reactions, but the skill we want to build for our children is to think rather than instantly react—to recognize how they feel, and *then* make a choice about how to act. This is a skill that needs to be explicitly taught. Repeat to your kids, "Feel your feelings. Choose your behavior." Role-play ways in which they might respond to hurtful comments, such as saying, "That wasn't a very nice thing to say" or, "I would never say anything that mean to you!"

Desire: Another very natural impulse that we see in young children is to want something someone else has. It might be a toy, or food, or a friend. Teaching children to share, to ask for what they want, and to use their words is part of helping them develop respect and esteem for others. Bullies lack respect for others and often think only about what they want. They also lack the social skills to get their emotional needs met cooperatively. Role-play asking a friend to share a toy or a treat, or asking to be included in an overnight being planned by a group of friends.

Jealousy: This is yet another powerful emotion that children need to learn to manage. Children may be jealous of another child's possessions, another child's friends or family, or another child's social abilities. They may be envious of how easily another child seems to make friends, or how well another child does in school. Jealousy is not only a very difficult emotion for children to deal with; it also diminishes a child's sense of his or her own value. Discuss the feelings that you see arise: "It sounds like you really wish you had one of those motorbikes; are you feeling jealous?" or, "I can see it is hard to always be in her shadow; does it make you forget how special you are, too?"

Power and control: These are also emotions that show up very early in life. By the age of three or four, a child may already be totally committed to being in charge, and other children may willingly allow the child to take charge. It is as important for the take-charge child to learn to share power in the group as it is for the more easygoing child to experience leadership and the ability to shape the direction of the group. Acknowledging the need to share power might begin with, "I know you like being in charge, and you have very good ideas, but it is important to take turns being the leader."

Identifying Individual Differences

All of these skills can be learned through modeling, by coaching on a situation-by-situation basis, and with daily practice. As Pamela Espeland, author of *Knowing Me, Knowing You,* reminds us:

- Each of us has our own unique talents, looks, and skills.
- We all have our own ways of doing things.
- We all bring something unique to our relationships.
- We all have our own patterns of behavior.
- People don't usually do things just to drive us crazy; they're being who they are. In fact, we probably annoy plenty of people just by being who we are!
- Getting along isn't about right and wrong or who is better or worse; it is about understanding ourselves and others.

Thinking about Pamela Espeland's ideas, consider these questions:

- How often do you talk in front of your children about other adults or children whom you find annoying?
- How do you respond when your children complain about other children?
- Do you compare your child to other children in a way that seems critical of others?

Your answers to these questions will give you some insight into how your children see your level of empathy.

DID YOU KNOW?

- The "prime time" for emotional and social development in children is birth to twelve years of age.
- Differing aspects of emotional and social development, such as awareness of others, empathy, and trust, are important at different times.
- Emotional attachment develops from birth to eighteen months, when a young child is forming attachments with critical caregivers.
- Emotional intelligence is shaped early on by experience, and forms the brain's emotional wiring. It is critical to life success.
- Early nurturing is important to learning empathy, happiness, hopefulness, and resiliency.

Teaching Empathy

Q: *"My preschooler is in an early childhood education program at our neighborhood elementary school. There are several children in wheelchairs. She is very curious and points. I have told her not to be rude, but I'm not sure what else to say."*
—Julie R., *mother of four-year-old*

SHERRYLL SAYS: *"This is a teachable moment! I am certain that the school could help you (and perhaps the other children in her class) learn about what it is like to operate from a wheelchair and perhaps why the children are in wheelchairs. There is no better way to develop respect and empathy than to have children actually talk with people who are different from themselves."*

Bullies see others as lesser than, inferior to, or worth less than themselves. The individuality, the value, even the humanity of the other person are out of touch for the bully. Thus, before bullies can learn to respect all other people, they must develop empathy, compassion, and understanding; in other words, respect comes with recognizing the individuality and humanity of others.

As Michele Borba, an expert on child development, violence prevention, and character development, points out in *Building Moral Intelligence:* "Empathy is the emotion that alerts a child to another person's plight and stirs his conscience. It is what moves children to be tolerant and compassionate, to understand other people's needs."

Teaching empathy, however, can be frustrating. You can't make children have empathy by saying something like, "You have to think about her feelings." You can't chastise or shame them into it by saying, "You made him feel awful." It's not enough to say, "I can't believe a child of mine would treat someone that way."

Empathy comes from the inside. It grows when children see how other people feel, when they feel what other people feel, when they "walk in someone else's shoes." Empathy is learned when you give your children words for what they are feeling, when you speak what they see other children reacting to, when you model for them actions that reflect the feelings and condition of others. This runs the gamut from saying, "I know how disappointed you are that you didn't win the game" to "I can see that she is very sad and lonely since her brother went away to school."

One common opportunity to teach empathy occurs when your child sees something happen to another person, such as tripping, falling, getting hit with water from a passing bus, or the like. These are all incidents that can bring about laughter and pointing. You can change the entire tone of their witnessing someone else's embarrassment or loss or accident by asking questions or making observations.

ROLE-PLAY: *Embarrassing Trip and Fall*

Ask, "What if you see someone trip and fall right in front of you? What would you say and do?"

ACTION 1: If your child responds by laughter and pointing, talk about how that might make the fallen child feel, and explain that it is not all right to make someone feel worse.

ACTION 2: If your child responds with sympathy ("Ouch, are you all right?"), suggest that your child help the child get up or help pick up their things.

ROLE-PLAY: *Your Embarrassing Trip and Fall*

Ask, "What about if you're the one who trips and falls? Is it embarrassing? What could you say or do to help get you through that moment?"

ACTION 1: "That was really embarrassing!"

ACTION 2: "I am such a klutz!"

ACTION 3: "I don't think anyone noticed."

DISCUSSION: Embarrassing moments are part of life. Maybe share a simple one you experienced. What is important is learning to deal with them graciously.

Learning to bridge embarrassing moments will come into play later when you teach your child how to advocate for others. A child who is able to see the discomfort of another child, or to feel the pain or embarrassment of someone else, or to sense the fear of another, is in a position to act. By identifying the feelings and vulnerability of others, your child will experience the desire to speak up for others, to speak out about mistreatment, and to intervene when witnessing bullying among his peers.

TALK WITH YOUR KIDS

- Has anyone ever said anything to you that hurt your feelings?
- Why do you think they did that?
- Do you think they knew that they had hurt your feelings?
- What did you say or do to them?
- Was it easy or hard to forget their hurtful words?
- Have you ever said anything mean to someone else?
- Do you think it hurt their feelings, too?
- Did you do anything to make them feel better?
- Is it hard for you to think about other people's feelings before you say something?

Teaching Tolerance

Teaching a child to value all people, no matter how different they seem from him or her, is both the challenge and the mandate of our age. It is this initial respect and then growing appreciation for the extraordinary range of people's shapes, sizes, colors, and cultures in the twenty-first century that will enable children to be both comfortable and successful in the world they are growing into. One of the elementary schools I work with in Denver has children from sixty-two countries. Large and small communities across the country are experiencing greater cultural and linguistic diversity, shifting our world and our worldview.

But, as Shanna Fox, a seventh-grade teacher at Discovery Academy in Tampa, Florida, says, "If you let students sit where they want, they self-segregate right back to their friends and comfort levels." Cooperative learning—structured activities in which students interact in purposeful heterogeneous groups that support the learning of all—is a powerful tool and an excellent way to direct discussions about tolerance and diversity in schools. Says Fox, "[Some students] wouldn't interact at all if it were not for me using cooperative learning. And because of it, they form friendships that stick . . . outside of their groups."

DID YOU KNOW?

- The 2000 Census reported that almost nine million children in U.S. homes speak a language other than English.
- The number of school-aged children who are English language learners increased 161 percent from 1979 to 2003.
- All fifty states in the U.S. now have English Language Learner programs in their schools.

Bullying that belittles or disrespects the language, culture, or customs of others is wrong. If you are a part of the dominant culture, your children will hear endless messages that reinforce the imbalance of power that comes with that position. Part of changing the culture of bullying is actively exploring differences, interacting with people unlike ourselves, observing and asking questions about likenesses and differences. This is a lifelong job for each of us, as adults, and for our kids. Look for opportunities to turn this from a "nice concept" into everyday action!

ROLE-PLAY: *New Haircut*
Ask, "What if kids at school are making fun of your haircut (or new coat or glasses or backpack)? What would you say and do?"
ACTION 1: Say, "That's not very nice."
ACTION 2: Say, "Yeah, whatever."

PAY ATTENTION TO: Body language, tone of voice, facial expressions, how it feels.

DISCUSSION: Do you think people think about what it feels like to the other person when they say things like this? Have you ever said something like this without thinking?

ROLE-PLAY: *A Child's Accent*

Ask, "What if your friends are making fun of the way another kid talks? What would you say and do?"

ACTION 1: Say, "Cut it out."

ACTION 2: Say, "Don't be mean!"

ACTION 3: Leave your group and go do something with the kid they were mocking.

PAY ATTENTION TO: Tone of voice, body language, facial expressions

DISCUSSION: Ask your child, "Have you ever done that? How did it feel? Has anyone ever made fun of you? How did it feel?"

TALK WITH YOUR KIDS

Following are some questions that will help you to explore your own ideas and beliefs and provide conversation starters with your children.

- What are the different cultures represented in your child's school? (Include categories such as ethnic groups, students with disabilities, new immigrants.)
- What characteristics first come to mind when you think of each group?

- What are the "messages" that you learned about differences when you were a child? What message is your child getting?
- Recall the incident in which you or your child first became aware of these differences. What was your reaction? Was there a discussion about it?
- Have your views changed since then? What efforts have you made to shape your child's views?
- Do you treat people differently based on these impressions? For example, how do you react when you see a teenager with tattoos and a cigarette?

Recall an experience when someone made assumptions about you based on a group you belong to. How did it make you feel?

Creating Opportunities for Cooperative Play

Q: *"My older son, who is five, has to have whatever toy someone else is playing with. If the toy is not being played with, it's not of interest to him. So when his younger brother or a friend is playing with anything, my son walks up and says, 'I want that,' and takes it. We've talked about sharing and asking and mutual respect and all the things we think we should be talking about, but his behavior hasn't changed a bit."*
—Daniel E., *father of five-year-old*

SHERRYLL SAYS: *"He is missing the step between the concept you are talking about and the actual behaviors. Begin by letting him know that this is a recurrent behavior you are seeing, and that it makes people unhappy. Role-play with him situations in which he wants something you have. Model for him how he should ask* *for what you have or ask you to share what you have. Then let him do it. Successive approximations are fine; he will probably learn this slowly. The next step comes with other kids. When you see a situation brewing, step in and help him be appropriate in asking for what he wants. If you need to intervene in a situation, you should first model for him the behavior you want to see from him, and then ask him to show you the proper behavior. This will be hard for him, so look for opportunities to reward him for appropriate interactions and sharing."*

As children become toddlers and have opportunities to play in the same area with other children, we begin to see hitting, biting, taking toys from another child, pushing, and the like. This is the time to begin teaching mutual respect and cooperative play. Direct and immediate intervention, saying something like, "We don't bite" is important at this point. Follow up with removal of the child if there is a second incident, saying something like, "If you bite, you can't play with the other children. You'll need to sit over here for two minutes, and then you can try again."

As children move from parallel play to cooperative play, around ages three to four, you will spontaneously see many, many opportunities for them to learn how to get along, how to work together, and how to resolve conflicts. Again, the issues are typically hitting, pushing, taking toys, messing up someone else's work, or biting. "Wait your turn" or "you need to share" should be consistent messages at this age. If the behavior continues, you can be more direct in your response: "You may not hit her because you want her toy. You need to wait until she is finished with it." If a follow-up is needed—and it often is—say, "You will need to sit over here for four minutes, and then you can try again to play peacefully with the other children."

Interlocking blocks or empty boxes are perfect vehicles for three- and four-year-olds moving from parallel play to shared projects. At this age; being present to encourage cooperation and to coach children on conflict resolution is more important than your participation in play.

Group drawing on a very large piece of butcher-block paper creates a perfect opportunity for transitioning into cooperative play. Allowing multiple children to work on one drawing immediately brings opportunities to make choices. Do they each want their own drawing area? If so, create some individual areas on the large sheet and reinforce the rules of play. This allows them to work individually, but in proximity, on the same piece of paper. If a child moves into someone else's section, it is an opportunity to talk about the rule you all made together, and to change or enforce the rule.

This also provides an early opportunity for preschoolers to experience contributing to a group project or product. This is an important early start in teaching the importance of being able to work with others, to cooperate, and, later on, to develop real teamwork skills.

The next step might be cooperatively creating a scene, perhaps a house with trees, animals, people, cars, and so on. You should acknowledge conversation that leads to cooperation and group harmony. You should also intervene with questions designed to help them problem-solve when there are disagreements.

> **ROLE-PLAY:** *Sharing a Toy*
> If your child grabs a toy from another child, model the correct behavior, and then let the child practice a better way.
> **ACTION 1:** Model by saying, "Can I play with that truck next?" Or ask, "Can we trade?" while offering up another toy.
> **ACTION 2:** Then let your child try it.
> **PAY ATTENTION TO:** Body language, tone of voice, and proximity to the other child.

DISCUSSION: Provide quick and easy coaching in your role-play and then lots of praise. If your child can only get a little bit of the correct behavior right, provide praise for that. There will be many other opportunities for your child to practice and get better at handling desire for what another child has.

If your daughter delights in pulling the dog's tail and watching him run, don't jump to the conclusion that she is being mean. For a preschooler, the big reaction is exciting and makes her feel very powerful. This is an opportunity to build empathy, to talk about the dog's reaction, and to model and then let her practice appropriate ways to play with the dog. Do not make the mistake of laughing at the reaction of the dog (no matter how comical it is) because this encourages her behavior.

ROLE-PLAY: *Petting the Dog*
When your daughter pulls the dogs tail:
ACTION 1: Get on the floor and model touch that the dog enjoys and finds soothing.
ACTION 2: If the dog is already skittish, letting her give him a snack and then gently stroking the dog will start to break the pattern.

Be a constant feedback monitor to acknowledge good behaviors and appropriate interactions. Be equally diligent about intervening and reteaching when your preschooler is misbehaving. Your consequences should be consistent and accompanied by as little negative emotion as possible. (Yes, you want to tear your hair out, but your anger and frustration have to model the very thing you want to teach!) Spanking is inappropriate and will only add to the existing problem—you can't stop aggression with aggression. Time-outs and logical consequences mixed with consistently catching and praising good behavior will get the job done. (See the Resources section for some books with helpful information about reinforcing your message.)

Elementary-Schoolers

As early as kindergarten age, the school starts to play a greater and greater part in shaping your child's relational skills and beliefs. This is the age when children begin to speak freely, and bullying becomes clearly evident. As Vivian Paley says so passionately in one of my favorite books, *You Can't Say You Can't Play:*

> By kindergarten . . . a structure begins to be revealed and will soon be carved in stone. Certain children will have the right to limit the social experiences of their classmates. Henceforth a ruling class will notify others of their acceptability, and the outsiders learn to anticipate the sting of rejection. Long after hitting and name-calling have been outlawed by the teachers, a more damaging phenomenon is allowed to take root, spreading like a weed from grade to grade.

As harsh as this behavior can be, it can be changed at this age, dramatically and quickly, because there is so much less "unlearning" to be done. At this age children are still trying out behaviors and responding quickly to both the reactions of their peers and the feedback of adults. Their behavior patterns are not as firmly fixed as they will be when they get older.

This is the age at which I have been most successful in building a culture of inclusion. Kindergartners know not only what bullying is but also how it feels to be the bully (pretty powerful actually, a heady feeling for a kindergartner). And they know how it feels to be made fun of, pushed around, or excluded. Kindergartners are astonishingly forthright in their discussions about their own school culture and equally willing to learn another way.

This is the age when I teach understanding of others' feelings, development of empathy, and taking responsibility for the impact that your words and actions have on the feelings and behavior of others. It is the prime time to teach advocacy, the important job of making sure everyone is welcomed and included, so no child is left out.

Cooperative drama is a perfect activity for developing mutual respect. It can be as simple as having kids see if others can guess a word they spell by making their bodies into the shapes of letters. They can act out their favorite kids' book. Some children at this age go into full production. The thing to watch for is equality of participation. Some children naturally emerge as leaders, but dictating what everyone else will do is not what we want. The goal is to encourage the "bossy" child to share the development process and to give everyone a chance to contribute.

SIMPLE GROUP COOPERATION ACTIVITIES

- Having one child start a story with a single sentence. Then the next child adds to the story, and on and on until it is complete.
- Making music together with various instruments or pots and pans.
- Planting: One child digs the hole, a second puts in the seeds, a third covers them up, and a fourth waters, and so on down the row.
- Baking a cake or making cookies.
- Making a bed (so much easier with two people).

Other strategies include giving feedback on how kids are problem-solving in their relationships and then redirecting them as needed, so they are more likely to be successful in a different activity. Acknowledging children who are being successful in working and playing well with others lets children know what behavior you expect.

And then, of course, there is role-play, the ultimate tool for modeling—actually showing your child what behaviors you're looking for. This is your best tool for clearly communicating your expectations, making them concrete and clearly visible. Using role-reversal, your child can demonstrate what s/he has learned in multiple scenarios. This is what cements the learning.

TALK WITH YOUR KIDS

Golden Rule: "Do unto others as you would have them do unto you."

- Have you said this to your children?
- How do you apply this in your life?
- What does it mean in your children's everyday lives?

Learning empathy and inclusion is a lifelong process. Simply deciding to be tolerant and loving does not make it instantly so. We have to work at practicing it in our interactions with others. This is a tough one to tackle, but it is one element at the heart of helping your children to avoid being bullies or targets of bullying. It is also at the heart of learning to live successfully in a world that is increasingly diverse.

DAY 3: SUMMING IT UP

The ability to identify a range of feelings in yourself and others is a precursor to developing empathy. Recognizing how it feels to have your feelings hurt, to want what someone else has, to desire power and control, to be jealous, are part of understanding human behavior.

Embracing the diversity of people is also a learned attribute. It goes hand in hand with recognizing, naming, and embracing individual similarities and differences. It develops as we help children to understand and respect that:

- Each us has our own unique talents, looks, and skills.
- We all have our own ways of doing things.
- We all bring something unique to our relationships.
- We all have our own patterns of behavior.
- People don't usually do things just to drive us crazy; they're just being who they are.

Remember that our words and our actions shape how our children see and relate to the rest of their community. Look for opportunities to discover and embrace individual differences in your own family as well as your extended community.

Communicating What You Mean, Like You Mean It

Q: *"My son has gotten in trouble several times in kindergarten for being 'abrasive.' His teacher says he bosses others around, has a tone of voice that sounds demanding, and doesn't have very good physical boundaries, which she explained means that he bumps into people. I feel like he is who he is. What does she want me to do?"*

—Craig E., *parent of five-year-old*

SHERRYLL SAYS: *"Learning social skills is a big part of going to school. You and the teacher should get together and talk about what social skills to target. He can learn to ask instead of telling. He can learn to use a less demanding tone. He can learn to pay more attention to other people and their things so he does not infringe on their personal space. Some children seem to pick these things up without direct instruction. Your child will benefit from direct coaching. He will be rewarded by kids who will want to spend time with him."*

From the time children begin to speak until they reach adolescence, our goal is to give them the skills to communicate clearly so they get the results they are looking for. Communication is how we let people know what we want, what we think, and what we feel; it allows us to share ideas or feelings with the people in our lives. But if we communicate in a way that alienates or offends, we will not be effective.

Children need to know that communication is not just about saying words—it's also about being able to anticipate how a message will be received. Verbal communication is clear—it is the words we say. Nonverbal communication is everything else, body language in particular. Since about 80 percent of what is communicated to others comes from nonverbal communication, it is critical that kids know what they are communicating so they can match their communication with their intentions.

Most children do think that communication is just talking. In fact, communication requires that the message that is put out be received, and that the person delivering the communication know that it is received. In essence, then, true communication is circular: you send out a message, the other person understands it, and you know they understood it.

This is central to the issue of bullying, because many interpersonal conflicts have their source in a failure to communicate. Likewise, the ability to resolve interpersonal conflicts and get relationships back on track also lies in the ability to communicate accurately and fully.

Verbal Communication

Verbal communication includes all the elements of word choices and how they are delivered. It includes tone, loudness, and pitch of voice. It includes where the emphasis is placed in speaking. The more children understand what they communicate—not just what they say—the more effective they can be in their relationships. For example, the child above may not have intended to come across as a bully, but if he is perceived as one and treated as one, he may begin to behave as one. Giving your children the best possible communication skills is central to the prevention of bullying.

DID YOU KNOW?

- The "prime time" for language learning is the first few years of life. Children need to hear caregivers talk, sing, and read to them constantly during these early years.
- Social knowledge and social skills determine to a large degree the quality and success of a child's school experiences.
- Children who feel secure enough to join, question, and listen to their peers and adults are the most able to interact successfully in a variety of circumstances and with a variety of people.

Word Choice

The first step in effective communication is to be clear about what you're saying in order to be understood. For example, toddlers can be effective in communicating that they want to be picked up by merely saying, "Up!" As they become preschoolers, however, we begin to ask them to speak in whole sentences: "Please pick me up." As they grow, we continue to teach them to use full sentences and to be increasingly precise about their communications. We teach them to take responsibility for communicating their needs.

In elementary school, children learn to write and speak with an increasing vocabulary. They need to continue to be accountable for saying clearly what it is they want, what it is they mean, and what it is they need. It is at this age that children mistakenly begin to think others will simply know what they mean, that others can read their minds or pick up on what is going on for them. Let kids know that friends and adults can't know what is going on for them unless they communicate fully—that is, unless the person they are talking to understands exactly what they meant to say.

Throughout this book, you will be teaching your kids to say

what they mean, to ask for what they need, and to communicate clearly. But the words are only the beginning. We need to build their total communication skills and, at the same time, give them insight into what they communicate unintentionally.

Voice

How else do we make clear what we want to say? The tone of your voice, the sound of your voice, and the volume and the speed of your speech all communicate additional things. For example, most parents hate whining. Whenever you catch your young child whining, it's a perfect opportunity to talk about tone and volume of voice, what it communicates, and what effect it has on others. For example, you might say, "When you whine like that, I find it so annoying I don't want to even listen to you. I need you to ask me for what you want without whining." Then be sure to praise your child's improved effort!

Children naturally develop communication and behavioral patterns that suit their comfort level. As a result, when you are trying to teach a new skill, there is often unlearning to be done. For example, children who raise their voice whenever they really want something will first have to learn that this is not an effective way to get what they want, that people are not responsive to this behavior. They will then have to "unlearn" this automatic response to wanting something, and "learn" to ask for what they want in a more acceptable volume and tone.

Certainly, any parent of a preadolescent or adolescent has either thought or said, "Don't use that tone of voice with me." And that same parent has probably experienced the wide-eyed child who says, "What tone?" Sometimes, this is the very moment to talk about the way they are communicating and what you're getting from them. Ask your child if that's the communication s/he intended to send. Most children are not naturally assertive. This is where role-play makes a difference.

ROLE-PLAY: *Voice and Emphasis*

Have your child repeat the following sentences, paying attention to the tone of voice, volume of voice, and emphasis on different words, and see how the meaning changes.

ACTION 1: Say: "Will *you* feed the dog now?"

ACTION 2: Say: "Will you *feed* the *dog* now?"

ACTION 3: Say: "*Feed* the dog *now*!"

ACTION 4: Say: "I'll walk the dog when this show is over."

ACTION 5: Say: "I'll walk the dog when this *show is over*!"

DISCUSSION: How does attitude get communicated in your voice? How does that change the way people react to what you say?

Nonverbal Communication

One of the most common concerns I hear from parents of elementary-school-age children has to do with their affective behavior. A parent of a nine-year-old describes her daughter as having learned all the right things to say. "She is able to ask for what she wants or needs, she can tell people how she feels, she can stand up for herself. The problem is she does all of this with her head down, looking at the floor. I've tried telling her to stand up tall and look me in the eye, but she doesn't get it."

Role-play makes it easy to teach your child the subtleties of nonverbal communication skills. As we demonstrate how to act in a given situation, children can experience what we are asking them to do, and then follow our lead. Through role-play they can bypass mental processing, which may include figuring out how to do what they are being asked to do and dealing with the discomfort of trying something new. Instead, they can move right into action. They can experience how the new behavior feels as well as their ability to be successful with the new behavior.

Following are the key elements of nonverbal communication that kids need to learn.

Eye Contact

Teaching children to look at the person they're speaking with is a critical aspect of clear communication. Making eye contact is one of the key ways we know that someone is speaking to us. Eye contact also tells us that the other person is listening. In short, it's a way to say, "I mean *you*." Likewise, it's the way in which children know that we are paying attention and that they can expect to be heard.

It is appropriate to ask your children to look at you when you're talking to them. It is also important to be aware of how well you listen, so that you can stop what you're doing and look at them when they're communicating something important. We can't do this all the time, but when it matters, kids need to know that we will listen. This is a critical part of building self-esteem. It says to the child, "You have value. What you have to say is important, and I am paying attention to you." Parents and teachers alike know what a difference it makes to crouch down so that you are at eye level with young children when you talk to them. It's tough on the knees, but it makes comprehension much easier!

> **ROLE-PLAY:** *No Eye Contact*
> Say, "Let's pretend that you want me to make you something to eat, and I am watching television."
> **ACTION 1:** While your child is asking, you can say, "Okay," but don't make eye contact or get up.
> **DISCUSSION:** "Did you know if I was listening, if I didn't look at you? How did it feel that I wouldn't look at you? Was it confusing that I was saying 'Okay' but not getting up?"

ROLE-PLAY: *Tickling*

Say, "Let's pretend that you don't like being tickled and I'm doing it anyway."

ACTION 1: Pretend to tickle your child. Say, "Now, I want you to ask me to stop, but don't look at me."

DISCUSSION: Ask, "Did I stop?" ("NO!") "Did you feel that I was listening to you?"

ACTION 2: Pretend to tickle your child. Say, "Now ask me to stop, look me right in the eyes, and move my hands away."

DISCUSSION: Ask, "Did that feel better? Why? How did the two ways feel different? Did one way work better than the other?"

TALK WITH YOUR KIDS

- Is it hard to get grownups to listen to you?
- What is the best way you've found to get an adult to listen to you when it's really important?
- What if you have something important to say, and the adult you tell doesn't believe you or isn't interested? What would you do?
- Has anyone ever accused you of lying when you were telling the truth? Do you have any idea why that happened? Do you think your body language or nonverbal communication had anything to do with that?

Body Language

Body language refers to all of the ways in which we communicate with the position of our bodies. For example, *posture* says something about how you feel and about what you are saying. If you say, "I really feel fine," while you are slouching, doubled over, and looking at the floor, then there is an inconsistency between your body language and your words. From the time children are preschoolers, we can ask them to stand up and look at us when they are speaking.

We can also begin to teach them about *comfort zones,* the distances people keep between themselves. Typically, we are more comfortable with close proximity to family members and good friends than to strangers. Teaching about comfort zones gives kids permission to use their own internal cues about people they're comfortable with or uncomfortable with, allowing them to move away from people who make them uncomfortable.

> **ROLE-PLAY:** *Personal Space*
> If your child pushes another child away because he is too close, role-play and then have your child practice.
> **ACTION 1:** Have your child say, "This is my space."
> **DISCUSSION:** Practice doing this, so your child can say it assertively while making eye contact. If your child says it petulantly or aggressively, practice so s/he experiences saying it clearly, without attitude.
> **ACTION 2:** Model and then have your child say, "Do you want to play?"
> **DISCUSSION:** Help your child to see that another child's actions might be an awkward request to join an activity. This builds empathy and social skills.

Gestures are another form of body language that tells us something about how or what the person speaking to us feels. Make a game out of asking your children what gestures mean. For example, when your arms are folded across your chest, ask them if they think you're receptive to giving them something they're asking for. If your arms are waving around wildly or you're rubbing your hands together or shaking your fingers, what do these gestures tell them about your mood or what's going on with you? If you're rubbing your neck or rubbing your face or twisting your fingers, what do they think it means? Give your children feedback on their body language as well, and explain what it reveals about what they are feeling as opposed to what they are *saying* they are feeling.

One parent I met teaches her kids about body language when they watch TV. She turns the sound off on the television and asks her children to guess what the characters in a show are thinking or feeling based on facial expressions, gestures, posture, and the like.

ROLE-PLAY: *Clean Your Room*
Ask, "What if you want to go to a friend's house, and I ask you to clean your room first? Show me how you would say, 'I'll do it later' with the worst attitude."

ACTION 1: Have your child act out with attitude, "I'll do it later!"

DISCUSSION: Ask, "What was your body language? What did it say that your words didn't say? What happens if your body language says something different than your words?"

ROLE-PLAY: *Giving Up Your Bus Seat*
Say, "What if a boy who rides on the bus confronts you and tells you that you have to give him your seat? What would you say and do?"

ACTION 1: You tell him "No," but your body language says you are afraid of him. What would that look like?

ACTION 2: You tell him "No" sitting up tall, looking straight at him; your voice is firm and clear. Then you go back to doing what you were doing. What would that look like?

DISCUSSION: Ask, "Which felt better? Which do you think would work better?"

Think about a situation where your child has behaved badly and is trying not to get in trouble. How many times have you said, "The guilt's written all over your face?" *Facial expressions* tell us a lot about how a person feels when communicating with us. This is important for children to know. Mixed messages occur when the words coming out of our mouths don't match our facial expression or body language. You can play a game with your children to see if they can guess the expressions on your face or portray an expression on their faces.

When they're old enough to read words on a card, have them demonstrate the facial expressions and body language that would be associated with the following emotions: happiness, fear, disgust, anger, boredom, surprise, determination, confusion, worry, and pride. Just for fun, try reading the faces of people you see in the grocery store, at the post office, in the doctor's office, or at your child's school. See if you and your child agree on the emotions that are being portrayed in the expressions of people you see.

The chart on the next page helps children understand what other people see in their body language.

BODY LANGUAGE	POSITIVE	NEGATIVE
Posture	Relaxed, comfortable, facing the other person, leaning toward the other person	Stiff, nervous, abrupt or threatening movements, turning away from the other person
Facial Expressions	Open, friendly, smiling, maybe serious or thoughtful depending on the situation	Blank, scowling, frowning, yawning
Eye Contact	Looking at the other person without staring, showing interest in the other person	Avoiding the other person's eyes, looking around, rolling your eyes, frowning
Arms	Relaxed, uncrossed	Folded tightly in front of you
Head	Nodding to show that you ag ree, tilting your head to show interest, and responding to the other person	Holding your head rigid, shaking your head "no"
Gestures	Talking with your hands shows interest and animation, involvement with the conversation.	Folding your hands and staying very still may show boredom or disinterest. Playing with something, like a paper clip, may show disinterest.

Adapted with permission from Knowing Me, Knowing You: The I-Sight Way to Understand Yourself and Others

What Do Bullies Communicate?

> **Q:** *"My daughter is very verbal and pretty controlling. She always says what she thinks, what she wants, and how she thinks things should go. People don't always appreciate her directness, and she has been called a bully. I want her to feel free to speak her mind and be assertive. At the same time, I want her to learn to listen and to respect the ideas of others. How can I accomplish both?"*
> —Andrew Z., *parent of eight-year-old*

> **SHERRYLL SAYS:** *"You want to look carefully at whether this is just a communication problem, or if her wanting to have things her way, combined with the way she presents herself, has crossed over into bullying. If she needs to be center stage, if she insists on things going her way, or if she is openly intolerant of others, you should begin to intervene now. She needs to learn to share being the center of attention, to share ideas, and to value the contributions of others. Teach her how to listen more, talk less, and use her strong social skills to bring out the best in others."*

One of the ways we can help children narrow down their understanding of bullies is to look at the way some bullies present themselves. Terrence Webster-Doyle, author of *Why Is Everybody Always Picking on Me?*, has an illustrative description of characteristics that can help children identify the signals that bullies give. To prepare for this discussion, get a large piece of paper and make a bubble for each of the following categories: Facial Expressions, Body Language, Words, and Actions. Brainstorm with your child and write into the bubbles the things you might see in a bully. This provides a concrete way to look at all the elements of communication. The illustration will give you some ideas if your child needs coaching to get started.

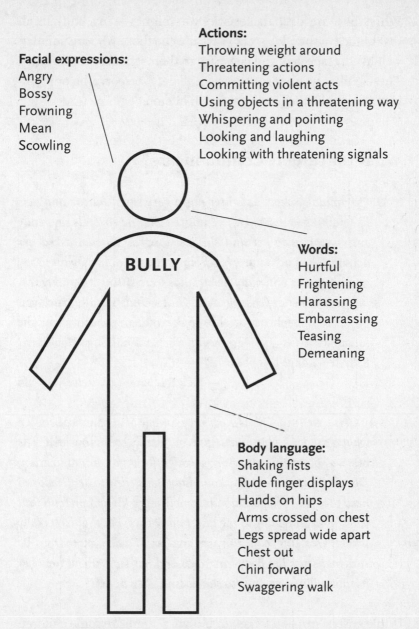

Facial expressions:
Angry
Bossy
Frowning
Mean
Scowling

Actions:
Throwing weight around
Threatening actions
Committing violent acts
Using objects in a threatening way
Whispering and pointing
Looking and laughing
Looking with threatening signals

BULLY

Words:
Hurtful
Frightening
Harassing
Embarrassing
Teasing
Demeaning

Body language:
Shaking fists
Rude finger displays
Hands on hips
Arms crossed on chest
Legs spread wide apart
Chest out
Chin forward
Swaggering walk

While these are all characteristics you might see in a bully, recall that bullies in the adolescent years may be those who are popular, well-liked, respected, and powerful in their school or community. These bullies who appear to have it all defy stereotyping or profiling, and can be the hardest to catch or stop.

What Do Targets Communicate?

Q: *"My middle-school daughter has a very sweet nature and acts like nothing bothers her. I've noticed that her friends say really cutting things to her and she just laughs. When I asked her about it, she said it hurts her feelings but she doesn't want to say anything. The other day her friends were sitting around cracking jokes at her expense. I said, 'That sounds awfully cruel, you guys.' Their reply was, 'Oh, she doesn't care what we say, she knows we're just joking around.' She said nothing. How can I help her change this pattern?"*

—Jack R., *parent of twelve-year-old*

SHERRYLL SAYS: *" This is a perfect example of dissonance between what a child is feeling and what is outwardly communicated. The best way out of this situation is straightforward communication. Discuss and then role-play your daughter saying to her friends, 'I need to talk to you guys about something. I know I pretend that you can say anything to me and I don't care, but that isn't really true. It's starting to hurt my feelings, and I'd like you to stop.' Be sure to discuss her body language and her fears about how her friends will receive this, so she doesn't back down."*

While anyone can be a target for bullying, there are some children who may be more vulnerable for a number of reasons. While it's absolutely critical to communicate that no one deserves to be bullied, it is also extremely helpful for children to understand how they present themselves in the world. Children who understand social cues and who develop their social skills are more comfortable socially. With this understanding comes choice, allowing children to look at how changing some behaviors may reduce their likelihood of being a target for bullying.

Once again, taking a lead from Webster-Doyle, get a large piece of paper and make a bubble for each of the following categories: Facial Expressions, Body Language, Words, and Actions. Brainstorm with your child and write into the bubbles the things you might see in a child who feels unsure, lacks confidence, or is unfamiliar with his or her surroundings. The illustration on the next page will give you some ideas to get started.

It is also interesting to have children note in this body chart where they feel responses to a threatening or frightful experience (knees weak, heart pounding, stomach upset, etc.). By increasing your awareness of the characteristics of your own shy or socially uncomfortable child, you can begin to target specific behavioral and social skills to work on. It's important that your coaching not come across as a criticism or judgment about your child's personal style. Rather, these are all new skills that give children other ways to communicate, just like learning new vocabulary words. More social understanding and social skills translate into greater social comfort and flexibility.

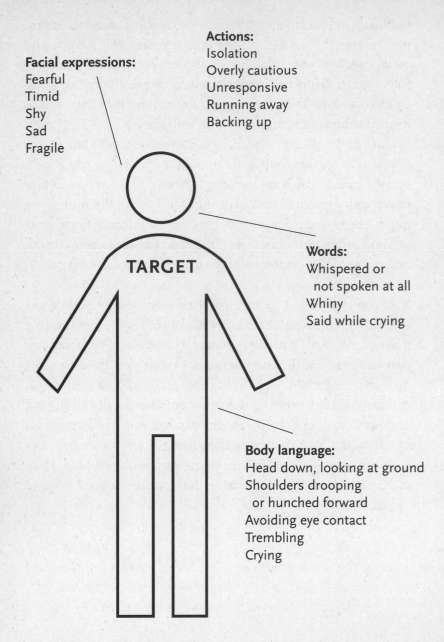

Facial expressions:
Fearful
Timid
Shy
Sad
Fragile

Actions:
Isolation
Overly cautious
Unresponsive
Running away
Backing up

TARGET

Words:
Whispered or
  not spoken at all
Whiny
Said while crying

Body language:
Head down, looking at ground
Shoulders drooping
  or hunched forward
Avoiding eye contact
Trembling
Crying

Communication: Putting It All Together

Children learn new ways of behaving, responding, and speaking one at a time. It is only with practice that they begin to put it all together. Patience and coaching are important to helping your child feel successful at each step along the way. This lays the groundwork for learning the next behavior and putting it into action.

Matching Words and Actions

Mixed messages can happen when words and facial expressions don't match, but they can also occur when someone says one thing and does another. For example, if the middle-school girl described earlier takes a joking tone and is smiling and laughing as she tells her friends that they are hurting her feelings, they will probably not get the message. Her body language needs to match the seriousness of her words. Children need to understand this principle—that words and actions that don't match cause confusion—in order to take responsibility for what they're communicating.

> **ROLE-PLAY: *"I'll Be There in a Minute!"***
> Have your child respond by saying, "I'll be there in a minute," in the following three scenarios. Have your child use different tones of voice and then talk about how the tone of voice changed the meaning of the words.
> **ACTION 1:** Your friend is about to leave for a ball game and you've run back for your glove. He calls after you, and you say, "I'll be there in a minute."
> **ACTION 2:** Your mother is trying to get you out of the house to go to the dentist, and you want to change your shoes for the third time, when she says, "Come on!" You say, "I'll be there in a minute."

ACTION 3: Your little brother asks you to come and help him get a toy out of the closet, and you're talking to your best friend about something important that happened at school. You don't really want to be bothered with your brother, and you say, "I'll be there in a minute."

DISCUSSION: What impact does your differing tone of voice have on others?

Timing

Timing is an element of effective communication that doesn't get enough attention. If people aren't prepared to hear what you have to say, it doesn't matter how clearly you say it. On the other hand, if kids aren't ready to tell you something, it can be almost impossible to drag it out of them.

It is important to teach children how to get someone's attention, how to tell if the person is listening, and when to speak. One of the ways to do this is to give kids feedback. "I'm not really listening to you right now." Or, "Please wait just a minute until I finish this, and then I will listen." When you are ready to listen, stop what you are doing, turn to your child, make eye contact, and be responsive to what s/he says.

If you teach your children the cues that signal that you are actively listening, it will pay off again and again. You will have laid the groundwork for respectful communication. Equally important, you will have established a family agreement that will prevent the endless preadolescent and adolescent "I'm listening," as they continue to play a videogame, send text messages, or watch television while you are trying to talk to them. Remind your child that communication only happens when the other person gets what you meant to say, verbally and nonverbally. Otherwise you're just talking to the air!

As kids get older, they may be more comfortable having a conversation where there is less eye contact and fewer nonverbal cues. This can happen easily while driving the car, taking a walk, playing a game, or sitting on the edge of the bed in the dark. This is when active listening and social cues, discussed on Day 5, really come into play.

TALK WITH YOUR KIDS

- Think about a recent conversation that didn't go very well. What do you think were the nonverbal communications that affected the way it went? What could you have done to change the tenor of the conversation?
- What if a bully is saying something truthful, but in an unkind way? For example, "You smell bad." Or, "You're always such a downer, can't you say anything nice about anybody?" Is there any way to give or receive this feedback so it is constructive?

Attitude

Attitude speaks volumes. Kids need to learn that through their words, tone of voice, body language, and actions, they are always portraying an attitude of some sort. It is not until late adolescence that kids are able to fully see that their presentation—be it haughty and disinterested, or warm, friendly, and accessible—affects everything that comes back to them. However, no matter how old your children are, your feedback can help them to develop an appreciation for the active and passive communication they transmit through their words, body language, and attitude.

For example, a positive attitude might be characterized by a friendly tone of voice, open body language, easygoing manner, and openness to communication. On the other hand, a negative attitude would be characterized by a sullen or angry tone of voice, closed body language, and nonresponsiveness or hostility.

When young people meet someone new, their attitude often determines if they have the possibility of developing a new friendship, or if they are ripe for being taken advantage of. How they present themselves determines how they are treated by teachers, coaches, the public, and people in positions of authority. By middle school or high school, the question "Why are teachers always picking on me?" may be answered by, "It's your attitude!"

> **ROLE-PLAY:** *Teacher Request*
> Ask, "What if your teacher asks you to go get your homework from your locker?"
> **ACTION 1:** You roll your eyes, mouth "stupid," without any sound, and walk out of the classroom.
> **DISCUSSION:** What reaction would you expect to get? Is that the reaction you want? What consequences would your response have? Is that what you want?
> **ACTION 2:** What if your teacher says, "If you want to have an attitude, just keep going to the office!" You respond with, "I don't have an attitude!"
> **DISCUSSION:** What is the consequence of your nonverbal communication at that point? Is it worth it?
>
> **ROLE-PLAY:** *Cooperation*
> Ask, "What if I ask you to go change your clothes for a meeting, and you say, 'Give me two minutes to finish this level of my game and I'm there!'"
> **ACTION 1:** Have your child repeat this in a friendly, cooperative tone.
> **DISCUSSION:** Ask, "How do you think I would respond to that? Is that just as easy as what we did before?"

The long-term goal is to raise young adults who realize the impact of the self they portray to the world, and who know they can choose how they come across. They may choose to change, stay the same, or ignore the entire issue. But what they should know is that most behaviors can be changed. By using the last two role-plays involving adult interactions, you can model the point that how you communicate has consequences. This lays the groundwork for discussing more fully the reactions of their friends and other kids they see in school or the neighborhood, and how they project to others that they might be a bully or a target for bullying.

As young people mature, they can observe what they are doing and the impact it has on others. They can learn to change as situations change. They can learn to be more conscious and fluid in their interactions. They can learn that their beliefs, fears, anxieties, and thoughts shape how they see the world and how the world reacts to them. The more they know about this reciprocity, the more choice they have about their relationships with others.

DAY 4: SUMMING IT UP

Children need to know that their thoughts, ideas, and knowledge are not communicated by osmosis. They need to be intentional about what they want to communicate, using all the tools they have at hand, including:

- **Word choice:** Being clear and precise
- **Voice:** Tone, pitch, volume
- **Facial expressions:** Eye contact, mouth, movements, smiles, frowns, grimaces
- **Body language:** Gestures, posture, speed of movement
- **Context:** Attitude, timing, readiness to listen

Communication is the act of putting all of these elements together so messages are clear rather than mixed. Only when children understand and can make choices about what they communicate nonverbally can they be thoughtful and deliberate about the impact their communication has on others.

Learning to Listen and Read Social Cues

Q: *"Why was I surprised when my daughter became a bully? She always wanted to be in charge. She always led the activities with her siblings and friends. She always thought her ideas were better. I liked that she was assertive and encouraged her to speak her mind. Then she went to school and everything looked different. She knew how to speak but not to listen. She knew how to lead but not how to cooperate and share ideas. She knew she had good ideas but she had little respect for the ideas of others. I'm now trying to play catch-up, to teach her how to get along with others without giving up who she is."*

—Cynthia T., *parent of six-year-old*

SHERRYLL SAYS: *"This is not an uncommon experience for bright, confident preschoolers. I would share your concerns with her teacher so you can work together to give your daughter opportunities to share leadership, to cooperate, and to listen as much as she speaks. She needs prompts from you, such as, 'Let Julie have a turn.' or 'Rich has an interesting idea, let's listen carefully so we know what he wants us to do.' She will pick up on these cues and learn to moderate her behavior."*

There are wonderful games to help kids learn to listen. I like to play a derivation of the old telephone game. If you have even a small group of kids, begin by whispering a phrase into the first child's ear. That child whispers to the next, and so on, until it gets back to you. It's usually a good laugh for everyone when they learn how different the ending message is from the starting message. Then, perform the activity again, but this time have each child whisper the phrase, and then have the receiving child whisper a confirmation of what s/he heard. The speaking child can confirm or correct, and then the second child can whisper it to the third child, who also asks for confirmation. This time, the phrase should be nearly accurate when it gets back to you. This is real listening.

One of the key ways in which children can better handle social situations is knowing how to actively listen and observe. For example, children need to know that active listening is not rolling your eyes, playing with your hoodie strings, shifting from foot to foot, looking around, yawning, or making comments to other people going by. Active and respectful conversation does not include constantly interrupting to give your own ideas, opinions, and thoughts. You cannot be an active listener and watch television, play a video game, or keep track of what is going on in your headphones at the same time. And it's hard to have a conversation if you're constantly distracted by your own thoughts—what you are going to say next, what a loser the person you are with is, or what other people might think about you.

These are all behaviors that will not serve your children. They signal disinterest, disrespect, and disengagement. Of course, sometimes this is exactly what kids want to communicate! But the important point is that disengaged behavior may not get the results they were hoping for.

Active Listening

Active listening means being engaged in a conversation, not just letting the words float by. Listening is one of the most neglected communication skills, yet it is the key to getting kids out of their own heads and into the world of other people and events. Only then do they learn how other people are different from themselves, how they think, what they want, and how they communicate.

Active listening is important for all kids, but especially so for those who:

- Are impulsive. It helps them stay focused on the speaker rather than thinking only of what and when they can say their piece.
- Are shy. It helps them to pay attention to the person they are talking to rather than their own unease.
- Have processing or learning differences. It keeps them paying attention to what is going on so they can interject appropriately.

Using the following steps, guide your child through a series of role-plays to build his or her skill and comfort level with active listening.

Active Listening Steps

1. **Show that you are in the conversation.** Make eye contact. Don't stare, but keep yourself connected by eye contact. For children who find this difficult, have them begin by looking at the person's nose until they become more comfortable with eye contact.

2. **Show that you are listening.** Nod or say something simple like, "Really," or "I hear you," or "Uh-huh."

3. **Be encouraging.** Say something like, "Tell me more about that," or "That's really interesting."

4. **Ask for clarification.** For example, "I don't understand that; can you explain it to me another way?" Or, "I've never thought about it that way; explain it to me a little more." You are checking to be sure you understood and to ask for more information.

5. **Reflect what you think the other person might be feeling.** "You must have been scared to death." Or, "I'll bet you couldn't believe your good luck!"

6. **Mirror what the other person is saying.** This shows the other person that you are listening, and understand what is being said. For example, "She really thought you were cheating on the test!"

ROLE-PLAY: *Parent Not Listening*

Ask your child to tell you about something that s/he did yesterday.

ACTION 1: Do not look at your child or respond in any way. Keep your hands and eyes busy with something you are reading or playing with or watching.

DISCUSSION: Ask your child how it feels to talk to someone who appears not to be listening.

ROLE-PLAY: *Reading a Book*

Select a picture book or newspaper article appropriate to the age of your child.

ACTION 1: As you read, ask your child to actively listen by:

- Looking at you
- Nodding as you read
- Responding appropriately with comments and then reflecting back what the story was about or asking a question about what you read

ROLE-PLAY: *Telling a Story*

Now ask your child to tell you the same thing s/he told you before or another story about something that s/he did recently.

ACTION 1: Use all of the elements of active listening:

- Looking at your child
- Nodding your head
- Responding verbally and then acknowledging a feeling or asking a question

DISCUSSION: Ask your child how it feels to be really listened to. Let your child know that it is the same for you, that you really like to know that s/he is listening when you're talking.

Listening to Your Inner Voice

I love teaching kids about their inner voice. Not sure which one I mean? It's the one saying, "What does she mean by my inner voice?" It's that voice in your head that has a running commentary about everything. While it lets us know what we are observing and what we should be paying attention to, it can keep us from listening to others because it is constantly yammering. As children develop, it is this inner voice that can begin to act as a conscience, helping them to choose between right and wrong.

It is also this inner voice that helps kids learn about social cues. When they say or do something, it is the inner voice that gives them feedback. For example, the inner voice might comment, "She doesn't look like she thought my joke was funny. I hope I didn't make her mad." Or, "He acts like I'm making him really mad. What was wrong with what I said?"

Taming Your Gremlin, by Richard Carson, is an excellent book for introducing kids and adults to the narrator in their heads. Carson teaches people how to listen, to notice the running commentary, the judgments, the criticism, and the doubts that are constantly introduced by the Gremlin. The illustrations are central to his message and give kids an entrée to the concepts that they wouldn't get with descriptions alone.

When you help kids pay attention to their own ways of thinking, they'll also begin to better appreciate how others think and act. This improves their ability to accurately read and understand what others are saying, which is central to getting along with others, as well as preventing bullying and conflict.

Observation: Another Form of Listening

Just as you need to understand how you react to things, you also need the ability to pay attention to the world around you and pick up on social cues. This skill, *observation*, is essential. But not everyone does it naturally. Teaching kids to observe and understand cues is fun and interesting. It is also important.

Social cues are all the verbal and nonverbal communications that people give out, knowingly or unknowingly. Kids need to be able to read and understand these signals in order to function successfully. They need to be able to interpret the signals of a person who is pretending to be nice in his speaking, but is actually menacing in body language. They need to be able to tell when someone is teasing or making a joke that is not meant to be personal or offensive, so they don't take it personally and overreact.

They need to be able to accurately read how people respond to their behaviors. For example, if their behavior is irritating someone, they need to be able to see the way the other person is responding and change their own behavior accordingly. Suppose your child's enthusiasm for school results in his waving his hand wildly in the air when he has an answer, and the teacher ignores him because she wants the behavior to stop. Some children will figure this out. Others will not, and may think the teacher doesn't like them. It is important to be explicit, to connect the dots for your child. In this situation, you might say, "Maybe the teacher wants you to simply raise your hand and wait for her to call on you, without making such a big show. Why don't you try that and see what happens?" If it works, continue to be explicit, saying, "Good. How did you know your teacher didn't like your earlier behavior? How did you know that she liked your new behavior?"

There are several everyday games I use to teach young children to observe. This is an important safety skill, as well, and will help you to know how astute your children are before you let them go off to play or walk to a neighbor's house alone.

Observation Games

Freeze

When you say "freeze," your child closes his eyes and tells you everything he remembers that was happening when he closed his eyes. Ask questions about color, size, people who are present, and any activities happening in the periphery. This teaches children to pay attention to more elements in their environment. It teaches them to observe things happening outside the thing they are directly observing. This is an important safety skill.

Take Something Off

You and your child stand facing each other and look at each other. Then turn your backs and take off two things (watch, hair bow, shoe, vest). Now turn back around and see if you can identify what the other person removed. Depending on the level of your accessories, you can do this several times. This teaches keen observation skills.

People-reader

Point out a person in a social situation, grocery store, movie line, or playground. Ask your child what she thinks the person is thinking or feeling, based on body language, facial expression, or tone of voice. Have her watch the person for a minute and see what clues there are. Most children can pretty accurately identify an emotion; what you want them to do is break down the elements of that emotion so they become more accurate readers. For example, a child might say, "I think he is mad; his face looks mean." This could break down further to: the veins are sticking out on his neck, his face is red, his eyes are bulged out, his body muscles look tense, and he is leaning over the person he is mad at. This degree of observation is far more useful, and later it can allow a child to distinguish frustration from anger, boredom from sadness, or happiness from mania.

Listening, Really Listening

Q: *"My children and I have an ongoing argument about what they now call 'multitasking.' When I ask them to stop playing a video game or listening to music or instant messaging on the computer so I can talk with them, they insist they are listening and can do two things at once. I don't think they're really listening. It feels really rude, and I find myself getting very upset."*
—Molly I., *parent of teenagers*

SHERRYLL SAYS: *"The evidence is really clear now that multitasking has been misunderstood. The more things you are multitasking, the lower the quality of each task. The same is true of listening. If you are doing something else, you may hear what is being said, but you are not really listening, and this is fertile ground for misunderstanding, miscommunication, and conflict. You should expect that they will stop what they are doing when you need to speak with them. At the same time, you need to be sure that you stop what you are doing when they have something they need to communicate. I suggest you go over the elements of active communication so there are some agreed-upon standards for your communication with one another."*

Conflict caused by a failure to listen is an everyday experience. How many times do you hear, "I told you I was going to Randy's after school!" You are equally certain that your child didn't tell you. This is a failure to complete the communication circle. If the person you are speaking to did not get what you said, then you did not communicate. Setting family guidelines for confirming communications will save you a lifetime of upset and confusion.

Incomplete communication is also at the heart of interpersonal conflict among children. When children get involved in a conflict, ask one child to explain what happened. Then ask the second child to tell you what the first child said. The second child will protest, wanting to tell you his version. Assure him that he will get a chance to do so, but first you want to know if he actually heard what the first child said. After the second child's version of events, ask the first child to tell you what the second child said. This teaches them to listen, even in the heat of the moment, so they have all the information they need to participate in the problem-solving process.

At another opportunity, you can follow up with questions such as, "Why do you think Bobby is frustrated?" "What does Angie want you to do?" "What made you so angry?" and "What do you think made her so angry?" You want to teach them to recognize another person's point of view in a conflict situation.

When children are able to communicate this clearly, bullying situations are more likely to be completely averted or resolved quickly. Children with these skills do not cower and back away from the affronts of a bully. They do not signal to the bully that they are a ripe target. They stand up for themselves, speak up for themselves, and read social situations more accurately.

DID YOU KNOW?

■ In a spoken message, 55 percent of the meaning is transmitted nonverbally, 38 percent is indicated in the tone of voice, while only 7 percent is conveyed by the words used.

■ Confident individuals listen to message content better than individuals who lack confidence.

■ People with less confidence in themselves tend to be better listeners for the emotional meaning of the spoken word—this is why some shy children are more attuned to the intended messages behind the words.

Understanding Social Cues

Q: *"My son isn't very good at understanding social situations and is pretty regularly teased. At first he thought the boys were teasing him because they liked him. So he responded with laughter and began hanging around the boys more often. The teasing got worse and turned into real bullying, egging my son on to do things that got him in trouble. Now my son sees that the boys don't really like him at all and is crushed. How can I help my son get better at understanding social situations?"*
—Brian C., *parent of nine-year-old*

SHERRYLL SAYS: *"This is a common problem for kids who don't read social cues accurately. Your son needs a more explicit approach to understanding how people interact, how they set personal boundaries, and how they respond to him. I would work with his teachers and begin to give him feedback and opportunities to role-play a wide variety of social situations. Talk about situations he encounters. Really listen to how he interprets what happens, and then follow up with other possible interpretations and ways in which he can be appropriate in his responses. This is a long process, but one that will be increasingly important as he gets older, particularly as he enters middle school."*

This young man is experiencing a common problem. While all children need to be able to pick up on social cues, to help sort out what's going on around them, children who do not do this well are prime targets for bullies. To make matters worse, children who don't understand social cues can develop significant behavior patterns that further set them apart and leave them feeling out of place.

Children who have difficulty with this may manifest one or more of the following behaviors:

- Anxiety, since they don't know what's really going on
- Inattention, since it's hard for them to pay attention to something they don't understand
- Rudeness, since they may not understand rules of conversation, such as waiting your turn
- Hanging back from peers, simply not knowing how to make conversation and relate
- Seeming "out of it" or "odd" looking
- Excessive interest in objects or books or drawings, since these are all more predictable than people
- Insistence on sameness and ritualistic behavior

From: www.pediatricneurology.org

Early intervention and explicit instruction in social cues and communication skills help to prevent these secondary problems.

TALK WITH YOUR KIDS

- Should people always say what they are thinking about other people? Why, or why not?
- How do you feel when someone says something really nice about you?
- Have you ever thought people were talking about you or making fun of you? Is it possible that you were wrong? How could you find out without causing an argument?
- Think of a time when you were really mad about something. Did you blame someone else for what was wrong?
- Why is it easier to blame someone else when things go wrong?
- Have you ever tried to figure out what part you played in causing a problem? How did it feel to see that you were partly responsible for what happened?

Overcoming Social Challenges

Your goal is to make the ins and outs of getting along with other people as transparent as possible, so your children understand what is happening around them and can respond appropriately. Kids who do not pick up on social cues, or who do not read other people accurately, are an easy target for bullies. This is a learning curve for all children, but it can be very difficult for some.

Children who have attentional issues, who are on the autism spectrum, or who have developmental disabilities often need more *explicit instruction* in order to accurately read social cues and understand social customs. By explicit instruction, I mean actually explaining how social situations work—for example, when a grocery clerk asks, "How's your day going?" Establish one or two responses, such as, "Great, how about yours?" and then give your child opportunities to practice in real life.

These children may be asked to do things that get them into trouble, or may be blamed for the actions of others. They benefit from a wide range of both discussion and role-play.

For example, one child was asked to show the kids on the bus what he had for lunch. He did and they proceeded to take almost everything in his lunchbox. The next day he again showed them his lunch, and they left him with one item. By the third day, he told his mother that he'd had no lunch. As he described the situation to his mother, his perception was that the kids were being nice, paying attention to him, and he wanted to be nice in return by sharing his lunch. He did not understand that he was being exploited. Direct instruction for this child included discussion and role-play. He needed a boundary, a rule, that he was not to open his lunchbox before lunchtime, and then he was not to share his lunch with anyone. He also needed role-play to be able to pull this off without being offensive or submissive with the boys who would expect him to continue to give them his lunch.

One of the things that makes it hard for these kids to "get it right" is that they often do not generalize from one situation to another. So the child with the lunchbox may learn how to handle that situation and then be willing to open his backpack for the same kids on the same bus. It is vital that parents and teachers continue to provide "transparency"—that is—clearly and explicitly explaining how social situations and people interact and work with one another.

There is also enormous pressure to conform, to be like everyone else. Children who are socially awkward often have distinct talents or interests. These may become a vehicle for bullies. For example, bullies might destroy a child's diorama or hide key elements of a drama costume or put soda in a child's science experiment. It is important to protect the ability of these kids to explore their talent.

Think about the kids who play dumb, who quit band, who stop participating in extracurricular activities because they are intimidated or bullied by their peers. Children who have distinct talents, whether it's writing, drama, art, sports, or chemistry, are often bullied into dumbing themselves down so they won't stand out.

This is why ongoing conversations about social expectations, social pressure, and conformity are so important. If your child suddenly wants to quit the band, it may not be for any of the reasons s/he is telling you. It may be that s/he is made fun of for carrying the instrument in its big bulky case around the halls of the school. Teaching children to stand up to the pressure to be different than they are is central to the prevention of bullying, as well as to building the confidence of each child as a unique human being.

At the heart of all these discussions about body language, assertiveness, social cues, and peer interactions is the goal of preventing children from sending the message that they are vulnerable. Practice and role-play are easy and fun ways for children to learn to be seen as they intend to be seen, as well as to better read the ways in which others present themselves. Armed with this knowledge, they can make better choices and be more successful in their interactions with other people.

DAY 5: SUMMING IT UP

As children become clearer about what they communicate (verbally and nonverbally), they are also able to see with more precision what others communicate, including mixed messages. This ability to read and understand the many social cues that guide how we interact with one another is crucial to building strong interpersonal skills and preventing bullying.

As kids pay more attention to their own ways of thinking, they'll also begin to better appreciate how others think and act. The key skills are:

- Learning to read people and social situations
- Observing accurately what is happening in social situations
- Asking questions about what they think is going on
- Talking to adults and their peers about how people learn to get along and work together

Active listening is an essential skill to help children be engaged socially, to make friends, and to be certain they are hearing what people think they are saying. The steps for active listening are:

1. Show that you are interested in the conversation.
2. Show that you are listening by nodding or simple verbal responses.
3. Be encouraging by giving feedback to the speaker.
4. Ask for clarification.
5. Reflect what you think the other person might be feeling.

6. Mirror what the other person is saying. Check for understanding.

You can accelerate this process by teaching your child to observe social interactions and be an active listener, and by having conversations that develop your child's ability to interpret what people are saying, through their words, their body language, and their actions.

Speaking Up for Yourself: Understanding Assertiveness

Q: *"My son has always been an excellent student, easy to get along with, a social leader. His first year in high school, he began to have problems with another student. It escalated until the other student hit him, giving him a black eye. When I went to the school, the principal said she would investigate. Unbelievable to me, she 'determined' that my son was making the whole thing up and had injured himself. My son was devastated and was unable to advocate for himself. He also insisted that I not get involved. Since that time, this other student has continued to harass my son. What can you suggest?"*

—Jason B., *parent of sixteen-year-old*

SHERRYLL SAYS: *"This really shows the lengths to which some schools will go to turn a blind eye to bullying. Given the physical abuse, you need to document all the incidents to date, as well as your communications with the school. You should write a letter describing this incident and request a meeting with the school administration to get a handle on this problem. If that meeting does not yield results, expand your correspondence list to include the superintendent and school board members. Your son has a right to be safe in school, and it is the job of the school to ensure that he is. At the same time, you want your son to improve his interpersonal skills and his ability to communicate assertively so he is able to advocate for himself in this situation. High schoolers are reticent to role-play, but they usually are responsive to a*

> *discussion about what they are communicating with their body*
> *language and behavior. Work on these elements first and then*
> *begin to build his ability to respond assertively. Since this is not*
> *a group bullying situation, your son can also use his friends*
> *and peers to reduce one-to-one contact with the bully. If there*
> *are further incidents such as the one you described, contact the*
> *police department."*

Kids don't automatically know how to be assertive, how to speak up for themselves, or how to continue to speak up in the face of adults who don't believe they are being truthful. Even in high school, kids need to continue to hone their ability to be assertive and persistent—and sometimes parents need to get involved to address an out-of-control situation. For both the young person and the parent, being skilled in dealing with highly charged situations assertively is an essential life skill.

On Day 3, you helped teach your child the elements of communication. Now, this chapter deals with the intention and attitudes that underscore communication. Building on skills introduced on Day 3, today we'll look at ways to help your kids be assertive toward bullies and overcome passive/shy or aggressive behaviors.

What Is Assertive Behavior?

Assertiveness is about directly communicating feelings, needs, or opinions without threatening or trying to manipulate another person. It is having the confidence to stand up for oneself. By definition, assertive behavior is appropriate behavior. As with many skills, the ability to be assertive is not something that children are born with. It is something they learn to do through trial and error and the reactions of people around them.

Kids can begin to learn assertiveness as early as preschool age.

You can accomplish this by modeling assertive behavior and by coaching them to be assertive in their own behavior. For example, if your children grab other kids' toys, you can correct their behavior, model for them how to ask if a child would like to share a toy and play together, and then coach your children to do the same with a confident and clear voice and demeanor—not bullying or pulling away.

As they get older, children increasingly need to learn how to speak up for themselves. When they are in grade school, they can learn to handle their own conflicts and problems. You might discuss, coach, and role-play at home, but then the goal is to have them advocate and speak up for themselves as often as possible through the elementary-school years. Even in situations where they need your backup, you want to let them take the lead in the discussion as long as they can. This builds confidence and competence that will enable them to continue to advocate for themselves in middle and high school.

You also want to role-play situations such as the one the young man at the beginning of this chapter experienced. What if you tell the truth and an adult doesn't believe you? How do you stand up to that self-esteem and confidence buster? One way to prepare for this is to role-play.

ROLE-PLAY: *I Don't Believe You*
Ask your child, "What if something happened on the playground and when you tell the playground aide about it, she says to you, 'I don't believe you'? What would you say or do? I'll be the teacher. Come and tell me about Johnny hitting you on the playground."
ACTION 1: When your child tells you, say, "I don't believe Johnny would do that!"
DISCUSSION: This usually stops kids cold, so you need to coach your child to tell you again with more details.

For example, "We were playing, Johnny wanted the
ball. When I said no, he hit me and took the ball."

ACTION 2: When your child tells you, again say, "I just
don't believe it. You must have done something to
him first."

DISCUSSION: Wait for your child's response (usually
another dead end!). Brainstorm how your child could
respond. For example, "Can you go get Johnny so we
can talk about what happened?" Or, "I know Johnny
always acts like he's innocent, but he is a bully on the
playground and I can't make him stop."

ACTION 3: Ask your child, "If she doesn't believe you,
who else could you tell who would listen and help
you?"

DISCUSSION: Brainstorm some ideas. It is important
that children know that there are other adults who can
help. In this case, your child could tell the teacher or
the principal. Kids also often think that parents can't
help with problems at school, so be sure to include
yourself in the list of people who can help.

ACTION 4: Then role-play being the second person your
child tells. Listen, ask a couple of questions, and then
agree to help. Offer to go with your child to talk to
the teachers.

The heart of this role-play is being sure that children know that
there are people who will believe them and help them. This
knowledge comes through discussion, role-play and experience.
Remember, assertive behavior takes care of your needs without
hurting someone else. It respects everyone involved. When children advocate for themselves, even in the face of disbelieving
adults, they are truly taking care of themselves.

SIGNS THAT YOUR CHILD EXHIBITS ASSERTIVE BEHAVIOR:

- Ability to speak up for himself when someone takes something of his
- Ability to be persistent if she asks a question that is not answered
- Ability to let go of slights or incidents that did not go his way
- Ability to share with others
- Ability to recognize and act on the feelings of others
- Ability to make eye contact when communicating
- Ability to use body language appropriate to communication
- Ability to use voice and language that are even and effective
- Ability to get her needs met without manipulation or excess emotionality

By kindergarten, it is astonishing how clearly many children can speak about what behaviors are bullying, who the bullies are, and which children will put up with anything without speaking up for themselves. By this age, children have a clear sense of who has power and who doesn't. They also have a strong sense of justice, which makes this an optimal age to teach assertive behavior. Children of this age are the most open to coaching on their behaviors, love to role-play, and are keenly aware of the results of changing their behavior.

In the early elementary years, there are daily opportunities to teach assertiveness. These years are filled with perceived slights, real bullies, adults who are not responsive, playground disputes, backseat arguments, and hurt feelings. Each of these is an opportunity to discuss and role-play ways in which children can stand up for themselves, speak up for themselves, and hold their ground. Success builds confidence, and this confidence enables your child to continuously build interpersonal and communication skills.

In the upper elementary grades, teaching and reinforcing assertive behavior is critical. Your child's experience of upper elementary, middle, and high school will be shaped in part by your child's perceived position on the social ladder. Developing skills that make children less susceptible to doing "whatever it takes" to feel safe, accepted, and comfortable in their school group is critical. Middle school has the highest incidence of bullying. This is also the age at which your child will be confronted with many choices and significant peer pressure about smoking, substance use, and other risk-taking behaviors. These pressures only increase in high school. The ability to respond clearly and assertively is paramount.

The assertiveness skills your children learn now will also determine their success in navigating relationships as they move into young adulthood. The ability to stand up to pressure in groups, pressure in dating relationships, and the pressures of college and young adulthood is most easily developed in these preadolescent years.

Aggressive and Passive Behaviors

Most children exhibit passive and aggressive behaviors from a very young age. In any playgroup, you will see children who take others' toys, who bite, scratch, or bully other children. You will also see children who passively take whatever is dealt to them or run to an adult, crying or complaining. Assertive behavior does not come naturally; it is learned from daily interactions and feedback, from the time children are able to interact with one another.

Aggressive behavior is stepping on the rights of others or imposing your will, beliefs, or actions on others. Aggression in behavior and communication is done without regard for the feelings or needs of others. It is self-centered, which is why you'll often see this type of behavior in toddlers, who are, of course, self-centered.

SIGNS THAT YOUR CHILD EXHIBITS AGGRESSIVE BEHAVIOR:

These early warning signs are only that—indicators that you should pay attention as your child develops:

- Feelings of being picked on and wanting to strike back
- Pattern of impulsive and chronic hitting
- Uncontrolled anger
- Generalized aggression and defiance
- Consistent violations of norms and rules; defiance of authority
- Pattern of intimidating and bullying behaviors
- Aggressive communication style
- Cruelty to animals, setting fires
- Covert behaviors such as stealing, vandalism
- Intolerance for differences; prejudicial attitudes

Stopping aggressive behavior in young children is something most parents attempt to do. We encourage them to share their toys, whether they want to or not. We explain that it is important to use their words rather than grab a toy away from another child. We don't tolerate hitting or kicking, biting or spitting. For the most part, however, children experience these limits as a hindrance to getting their needs met.

Teaching children to play together is a combination of limiting inappropriate behaviors, speaking the frustration they are experiencing that is causing the behavior, and modeling assertive behaviors. For example, "I know you want to play with the truck, but Chad had it first. Please give it back to him." At the same time, if need be, guide your child to return the truck and give him or her another toy.

DID YOU KNOW?

While all kids experience stress, those who are learning to be more assertive or less aggressive may be experiencing more stress, because all change takes energy and effort. The American Academy of Child and Adolescent Psychiatry recommends the following stress reducers:

- Exercise and eat regularly.
- Avoid excess caffeine intake, which can increase feelings of anxiety and agitation.
- Learn relaxation exercises (abdominal breathing and muscle relaxation techniques).
- Learn to state feelings in polite, firm, and not overly aggressive or passive ways (e.g., "I feel angry when you yell at me." "Please stop yelling.").
- Rehearse and practice situations that cause stress.
- Learn practical coping skills. For example, break a large task into smaller, more easily achievable tasks.
- Decrease negative self-talk: challenge negative thoughts about yourself with alternative neutral or positive thoughts. "My life will never get better" can be transformed into "I may feel hopeless now, but my life will probably get better if I work at it and get some help."

- Learn to feel good about doing a competent or "good enough" job rather than demanding perfection from yourself and others.
- Take a break from stressful situations. Activities like listening to music, talking to a friend, drawing, writing, or spending time with a pet can reduce stress.
- Build a network of friends who help you cope in a positive way.

Passive behavior, on the other hand, is allowing yourself to be stepped on. It is standing by and letting others take advantage of you. It is being afraid to speak up. It is putting others' feelings ahead of your own. These are all passive behaviors. Passive behavior often shows no regard for your own feelings or needs. It is also a way of putting the responsibility for what happens in your life in the hands of someone else.

SIGNS THAT YOUR CHILD EXHIBITS PASSIVE BEHAVIOR:

These early warning signs are only that—indicators that you should pay attention as your child develops:

- Discomfort in group situations
- Vulnerability to being taken advantage of by others
- Socially withdrawn
- General depression or disengagement
- Excessive feelings of isolation and being alone
- Talk of feeling rejected or friendless
- Lack of confidence
- Inability to stand up for oneself

Think of the child who silently puts up with aggressive behavior on the part of other children. We need to speak up on behalf of these children and teach them assertive responses to aggression. For example, bring the aggressive kid over and model a response for the passive child. Look the aggressive child in the eyes and say, "Stop it. I don't like that." Then see if the passive child would like to try saying this directly to the aggressive child. It may take modeling repeatedly for passive children to begin to speak up for themselves, but they will with time and practice.

While it may seem that most of this intervention is lost on the two- or three-year-old, it is the basis for continuing to teach effective communication and social interaction in the preschool years. It teaches children how to clearly communicate their needs. In fact, role-play is most successful with this age, because they have so little to "unlearn." It provides a safe outlet for them to express themselves and establishes skills that they will use for the rest of their lives.

Overcoming Passive Behaviors and Building Confidence

There are many young children who are quiet, shy, and unable to stand up for themselves. While this may be a predisposition, it is still appropriate and important to teach these children to speak up for themselves. Preschool is the time to begin teaching them skills that will enable them to advocate for themselves. This should be done simply and gently through consistent coaching and modeling. This might include:

1. If you notice your child passively allowing another child to take his or her toy, you might intervene and say, "It's all right to share, but she should ask you instead of just taking your toy."

2. If another child pushes your child down, you might pick your child up and say, "That doesn't feel good, does it?" Coach your child to say to the other child, "That wasn't nice. Please don't push me down."

3. If your child isn't participating with the group but would like to, you might take your child by the hand and say, "Do you want to play with the others?" Coach your child to get up and ask, "Can I play, too?"

Opportunities for socialization where you can stay, observe, and coach are invaluable. If you aren't already involved, join or start a playgroup, go to the park, hang out at the pool; give your child lots of opportunities to learn to be around other children before s/he goes into a preschool or kindergarten setting where s/he will be expected to know how to participate and get along. Look for a parent co-op preschool where there are lots of adults around and you can see and participate in your child's learning of social skills. Then begin to let go and allow your child to learn to negotiate socially with the help of a preschool teacher. While we place enormous emphasis on letter naming and knowing colors, some of the most neglected keys to success in kindergarten are the skills of interacting successfully with other kindergarteners, being a part of a group, listening, and following directions.

In the early elementary years, social situations, classroom activities, and family living provide consistent opportunities to teach your child assertive behavior through modeling, problem-solving, and role-play. At this age, children often interact inappropriately in front of us, without even thinking. Behaviors you're likely to witness firsthand include name-calling, bossiness, thoughtlessness, ganging up on someone else, racial slurs, and hate speech. It is pretty astonishing when you see it, but it is also the moment to jump in and find out what's going on. Ask kids how else the situation could be handled, and, if appropriate, suggest a resolution and have them role-play it. This strategy is also ideal for bickering siblings. The problem-solving skills they learn with each other will stay with them to adulthood.

ROLE-PLAY: *Party Invitation*
Ask your child, "What if your friend Sally has invited all the girls in the class to her party except you? What would you say and do?"

ACTION 1: Brainstorm and then have your child role-play "Sally, I feel really left out. Did you mean to invite everyone but me to your party?"

ACTION 2: Have Sally say, "Of course not, I sent you an invitation."

DISCUSSION: This is a good opportunity to talk about the importance of asking questions rather than making assumptions.

ROLE-PLAY: *Name-Calling*
Ask, "What if there's a guy who calls you 'retard' under his breath—but loud enough that other kids hear him—every time he gets near you? What would you say and do?"

ACTION 1: Stand up tall, look him in the eye, and say, "What? I didn't hear you!"

ACTION 2: Next time, stand up tall, look him in the eye, and say, "Can you say that louder!"

DISCUSSION: What we know about these kinds of harassment is this: The sooner you toss it off, the better you are at letting it slide off of you like you're Teflon, the faster it will go away. This kind of bullying is no fun if the target doesn't get upset! Try it and see.

ROLE-PLAY STEPS TO DEAL WITH NAME-CALLING:

1. Communicate clearly and simply, including body language, voice, and eye contact.
2. Keep a respectful distance between the child and the bully.
3. Do not touch or threaten each other in any way.
4. Practice, practice, practice.

What about Tattling?

As someone who works in the field of prevention of child abuse, one of the biggest battles I've faced has been teaching children that telling an adult about a problem is not tattling. Kids will keep secrets about a friend being bullied or abused because they don't want to "tattle." It is important to establish as early as possible that this is not tattling.

Tattling is telling on another child or sibling *so you can get them in trouble!* Telling because you or another child needs help is not tattling. It is being a responsible friend. Children who are bullied often lack the skills to advocate for themselves. Since other children often know about bullying before adults do, telling an adult in order to get help is something your children should feel comfortable doing.

ROLE-PLAY: *Stolen Lunch Money*
Ask your child, "What if you know that another kid in our neighborhood is being bullied? Let's say an older boy takes his lunch money every day. What would you say and do?"

ACTION 1: Meet the kid and walk to school with him (safety in numbers).

ACTION 2: Advise the kid to walk to school another way (avoidance).

ACTION 3: Tell a grownup so the bullying behavior can be addressed.

DISCUSSION: Who would you tell? Isn't that tattling? What do you think they could do? (The most common answer from children is that the adults will do nothing.) What if that adult didn't do anything? What would you do next? (A combination of the three responses may be the best solution.)

ROLE-PLAY: *Advocating for Another*

Ask, "What if you know that a girl in your class is terrorizing another girl by leaving her threatening notes and getting other girls to treat her badly—and then pretending to sympathize with the girl she is targeting? What would you do?"

ACTION 1: Leave a note for the teacher telling her what is going on (an attempt to remain anonymous).

ACTION 2: Talk to a counselor or parent and ask what to do.

DISCUSSION: Is this tattling? Why, or why not?

ACTION 3: Speak to the ringleader directly. Tell her that her behavior is cruel and she needs to stop. (This step is an option only if your child has high standing on the social ladder and feels confident enough to exert her influence.)

Overcoming Aggressive Behaviors

Since most bullying takes place when children are unsupervised or loosely supervised, elementary schools are filled with bullies and targets. Schools know this, and many elementary schools pay lip service to having a "No Bullying" program. They put posters up in the halls and classrooms. They may even have a written policy. But very few elementary schools do what needs to be done to change the culture of bullying. This matters, because feeling safe in school is a prerequisite for learning. Schools need a combination of supervision, direct instruction in the ethical treatment of others, and policies that provide for resolving interpersonal conflicts successfully.

If you hear a teacher say something like, "They have to learn to work it out," you know that this teacher either doesn't fully understand the problem or doesn't know how to deal with the problem effectively. If kids knew how to work it out, they would have done it already!

School-age children need to learn:

- Social norms for being with other people (they may be different in school than they are in the neighborhood, but they have to be learned)
- How to solve interpersonal problems
- How to advocate for themselves and others
- Where to go and whom to talk to about problems
- That they will be heard and believed
- That action will follow to remedy the problem

In the following role-play situations, you want to find out what skills your child is bringing to the table. There will be more refinement later. For now, pay attention to how much they already know about speaking up and advocating for themselves.

ROLE-PLAY: *Lunch*

Ask your child, "What if a new kid at school takes part of your lunch without asking? What would you say and do?"

ACTION 1: "That's my lunch, please leave it alone."

ACTION 2: "If you want to trade, let me see what you've got."

ACTION 3: "We have a rule against trading food. Please give that back."

DISCUSSION: What is your family rule? Is there a school rule? Would your child tell the teacher the first time this happens, or try to handle it alone?

ROLE-PLAY: *Don't Push Me*

Ask, "What if a boy pushes you down on the playground? You ask him to stop, and then he does it again a few minutes later. What would you say and do?"

ACTION 1: "That's not nice, don't push me."

ACTION 2: "Do you want to play ball? I'll go get one."

ACTION 3: "That hurt. I'm going to get a teacher if you don't leave me alone."

PAY ATTENTION TO: Tone of voice, eye contact

DISCUSSION: How does it feel to stand up for yourself? Do you think this would work?

ROLE-PLAY: *Tapping Chair*

Ask, "What if the girl who sits behind you keeps tapping the bottom of your chair with her foot while you're taking a spelling test, because she knows it bothers you? When you ask her to stop for the third time, the teacher tells you not to talk during the test. What would you do and say at that moment?"

ACTION 1: "I was asking her to stop kicking my chair."

FOLLOW-UP QUESTION: "What would you do and say later?"

ACTION 2: "I wasn't cheating on my test; I was trying to get her to stop kicking my chair. She does this to get me mad, and I don't know how to make her stop."

PAY ATTENTION TO: Tone of voice, ability to articulate the problem and the request for help

Retraining Reactive Kids

Recognizing habitual responses is especially important when we are teaching kids how to be more assertive or less aggressive. A reactive child is one who, for example, habitually responds with anger or by striking out when someone looks at him in what he perceives to be an aggressive way. Or, a reactive child might respond to being confronted by hanging her head and looking away. These are behaviors that can become automatic in early childhood and can lead to bullying or submissive behavioral patterns. Once these patterns of behavior are noticed, they can be unlearned.

One of the ways I work with bullies is to set boundaries and then role-play practicing those boundaries again and again. For example, with kids who fly off the handle or over-react when simple things happen, like being bumped by someone else, I would set this boundary: you do not get to react negatively to this; you get to say, "Excuse me" and keep moving.

I do not want to make this sound too simple. For a child who reacts automatically, this is a completely impossible concept. But role-playing is the key! I will actually role-play bumping into him. He will respond emotionally as he always does, but I then ask him to follow my instructions, to disengage, to say, "Excuse me" and move on. Then we do it again, and again, and again.

Once he's gotten pretty good at doing it with me, I ask another child to be in the role-play. Interestingly, it is almost like starting over for the bully, because it is another child bumping into him rather than an adult. Again, I ask that he follow the instructions until he can do the role-play without feeling activated emotionally. This is nothing more than unlearning an inappropriate response. It is hard work to change a behavioral pattern, so it is critical that children be acknowledged and praised for the new behaviors they are developing!

For kids who are bullies, there are many triggers that may need to be unlearned. If your child struggles with reacting to triggers, pay attention to what immediately precedes a reaction, notice patterns, and then begin to role-play those situations. It will take time for your child to develop new ways of reacting, but the payoff will be lifelong!

A similar method can be used with children who have difficulty being assertive, who are uncomfortable speaking above a whisper, or making eye contact, or asking for what they need. I develop a role-play that requires the child to say in a very loud voice, "Look at me!" Another role-play would have the child squeeze my arm to get my attention, as s/he says in a very assertive tone, "I need to talk to you." While this won't be the final desired way of communicating, going overboard—sometimes to the point of ridiculousness—gives the child an experience of being heard, of being powerful, of being demanding.

Some very soft-spoken children can't speak in a louder voice unless I do it with them. So we yell together. If necessary, we go to an empty playground and really yell together. Then I go to one side of the park, the child goes to the other, and we have a yelling conversation. Just the experience of feeling "bigger" can change their self-concept enough that children can begin to learn the communication and assertiveness skills that will be essential, not only to their lives, but to reducing their likelihood of being a target of bullying.

TALK WITH YOUR KIDS

- How does it feel to be passive, to let someone take advantage of you or push you around?
- How does it feel to be aggressive, to take advantage of someone else?
- How do you think the other person feels when you are aggressive?
- How do you think the other person feels when you are passive?
- How does it feel to be assertive, to be clear and straightforward in saying what you mean?
- How does it feel when other people do that with you?

Three Assertiveness Lessons

1. It's Okay to Say No

Of all the skills most people never learn, this is the big one! You probably struggle with it yourself. We live in a culture that encourages us to share, to be helpful, and to get in there and participate. Not a bad thing. What's missing is the assertiveness part. Remember, assertiveness is grounded in respect for others *and* respect for yourself.

This is another behavior we can model for our children. For example, another parent calls and asks you to take on the classroom party because she has overbooked herself. Would you be able to say, "I really wish I could, but I have another commitment"? Or would you take on a volunteer effort that stretches you too thin, in order to be the *parent who could?*

Actively work with your kids, as they grow up, to develop their ability to say no. They can be kind and polite and considerate of other people's feelings, but they must learn to say *no!*

2. Make Choices, Don't Give Them Away

One of the places we see a lack of assertiveness is in making choices—or in not making choices. It's interesting how we give our choices away, or manipulate people into doing what we want them to do, without clearly saying what we want. We've all been in this scenario before! A friend invites you out to lunch and asks where you would like to eat. You answer, "Oh, I don't care." Then, when your friend suggests Chinese, you respond, "Let's not do Chinese." When she suggests Thai food, you respond, "Not Thai." Finally she says, "All right, the Old Hat Diner will have to do!" In essence, you have given your choice away by not choosing, or you have gotten what you wanted in a covert manner.

The opportunity to teach children how to make choices begins around the age of two. In fact, this stage is known as the terrible twos because that's when children learn that there is yes, and there is no. This is the opportunity to teach children how to make choices. For example, instead of asking, "Which dress do you want to wear?" ask your child, "Do you want to wear the red dress or the blue dress?" This gives your child a choice with limits and builds her own capacity to make choices.

Children also need to learn to express choices when they're play-ing with one another. Some children naturally take the lead, saying, "Let's go play house," or, "Let's go play baseball." It's important to teach these natural leaders to give more reticent children the chance to choose and, in fact, to encourage them to choose.

On the other hand, we often hear children who are not very

good at expressing their preferences, saying "I don't care." This is your cue to talk about how this gives their choices to others. For example, if you ask your child what she wants for lunch and she says, "I don't care," offer baked worms! Then you can talk about what happens when you "give your choice away" by not making a choice.

3. Ask for What You Want

Children often act as though we can read their minds, as if we know what is going on for them, and we know what they want or need. Asking for what you want or need is another skill we need to teach. Many children get the message that the needs of others are more important than their own needs. Many adults do not feel comfortable asking for what they need, so teaching children to ask clearly and appropriately for what they need is a learning opportunity for everyone. Again, modeling is a wonderful way to teach this skill. For example, if your children interrupt you while you are on the phone, it is instructive to say to them, "It is upsetting to me to be interrupted when I am on the telephone. If it is not an emergency, please raise your hand. If I can stop and see what you need, I will. If I can't, please do not interrupt me."

Another important way to teach this principle is by coaching children to speak up for themselves. For example, when your child has an issue with a teacher, you are probably inclined to jump right in, head for the school, and deal with it. In preschool this might be the appropriate response. But as your child gets older, it is far more instructive to talk with your child about ways to handle the situation, and then to go along to support his/her handling of the problem with the teacher.

> **ROLE-PLAY:** *Take Out the Trash*
> Ask your child, "What if I ask you to take the trash to the curb, and you're in the middle of doing your home-

work? Show me three responses: aggressive, passive, and assertive."

AGGRESSIVE: "I'll do it when I'm good and ready."

DISCUSSION: What body language goes with this response?

PASSIVE: "All right." You stop in the middle of a problem to take the trash out.

DISCUSSION: What body language goes with this response?

ASSERTIVE: "I need to finish this problem, and then I'll take it out."

DISCUSSION: What body language goes with this response?

ROLE-PLAY: *Putting Towels in the Bin*

"Your coach gets on you for not putting the towels in the locker room bin, but it's not your assigned day, it's Jack's. Show me three responses: aggressive, passive, and assertive."

AGGRESSIVE: "It's not my job; you'll have to find somebody else."

DISCUSSION: What body language goes with this response?

PASSIVE: It wasn't your job, but you quietly pick up all the towels and put them in the bin.

DISCUSSION: What body language goes with this response?

ASSERTIVE: "I think it's Jack's responsibility. I'll find him and we'll get it done."

DISCUSSION: What body language goes with this response?

ROLE-PLAY: *Bicycle in the Driveway*

Ask, "What if your father is angry because your bicycle is in the driveway when he comes home? Your brother left it there. Show me three responses: aggressive, passive, and assertive."

AGGRESSIVE: "It's not my problem."

DISCUSSION: What body language goes with this response?

PASSIVE: You say, "Whatever," and you put the bike away.

DISCUSSION: What body language goes with this response?

ASSERTIVE: You say, "John left it there, but I can put it away."

DISCUSSION: What body language goes with this response? Can you think of some situations from your life when you acted in one of these ways, but now you see another way you could act?

DAY 6: SUMMING IT UP

Assertive behavior is by definition appropriate behavior. It is behavior that respects oneself and others. It is direct communication of feelings, needs, or opinions without threatening or trying to manipulate another person. It is the ability to stand up for oneself. An assertive child is able to:

- Speak up for self and others
- Be persistent if a question is not answered
- Let go of slights or mistakes
- Share with others
- Recognize and act on the feelings of others
- Make eye contact when communicating
- Use body language appropriate to communication
- Use voice and language that are even and effective
- Get needs met without manipulation or excess emotionality

Learning to be assertive rather than passive or aggressive is a key element of successful communication and relationships. When you notice your child responding in an assertive way that is particularly effective, say so! When you notice your child responding passively or aggressively, call a time-out and ask for an assertive response. Provide coaching as needed, and remember all the nonverbal components that go into communication.

Resolving Conflicts:
When a Bully Shows Up

Q: *"Our son is nine years old and in the third grade. He has never had a behavioral or academic problem in school, until now. We recently found out that he was being called names like 'fag' and 'retard.' We talked to his teacher, and the bullying seemed to decrease for a while. He didn't tell us when it started again or when it escalated on the playground. Only when he started to be sick every morning, begging not to go to school, did we get the whole story. Even while we were trying to work with the principal to get it resolved, the bullying continued. I know he needs more skills to protect himself. What can we do?"*
— Janis D., *parent of third grader*

SHERRYLL SAYS: *"This is every kid's fear, that telling will only make the bullying worse. This is a real fear, because this really happens pretty regularly in schools that do not have a comprehensive approach to bullying. The bully gets called into the office, he learns who 'ratted him out,' and he makes sure they never do it again. When this happens, the targeted child is afraid to tell again, and the bullying continues. At this point, you and your son need to go to the school and help the school understand how their handling of the situation made things worse. Your child needs to be protected from being in isolated situations with the bully—maybe there is another child who could act as a buddy for a while. You should also be really open with your child about the fact that things got worse at first and about why it is still important to ask for help again. At the same time, you want to continue, through role-play and discussion, to build his capacity to speak up for himself, to use all of the assertive communication and behavioral skills, and to practice his conflict resolution skills."*

We can do everything in our power to protect and prepare our kids, but bullying will still be out there, in the lunchroom, the bathrooms, the corners of the playground, and the neighborhood. Today, you'll give your child specific techniques—like "ignoring" strategies and comebacks—to solve conflicts and peer-to-peer problems without escalating a situation.

Parents As Coaches: How to Mediate Conflicts with Your Children

Conflict is a part of life. We will never be without it and, in fact, we consistently learn from conflict. When conflict occurs among children, it is our opportunity to:

- Focus on the solution, not who is at fault
- Help them define the conflict
- Practice generating ideas to resolve the conflict
- Learn to recognize the feelings generated by the conflict
- Identify their reactions to others involved
- Choose an option to resolve the conflict

The patterns young children develop in response to conflicts tend to be positive or negative. They may learn to escalate the conflict through harsh words, threats, and physical aggression, or they may learn to use conciliatory, respectful language and empathy to de-escalate situations and find mutually satisfying outcomes. Both are learned behaviors.

You can help your children be more effective in handling conflicts by being active listeners and problem-solving coaches. Numerous studies have found that parents who listen, who encourage their children to talk about a problem, who ask for specifics and brainstorm possible solutions have kids who are better equipped to handle conflicts themselves in the future.

All the skills learned throughout this book reinforce each other. Children who have effective conflict resolution skills tend to have more positive self-concepts connected with learning self-respect, empathy, cooperation, and communication skills. And as with most skills, conflict resolution skills are best learned through experience. Fortunately, children give us plenty of opportunities to teach them. Begin by choosing small conflicts. If you have more than one child, these present themselves daily. If not, watch for a squabble between your child and a friend. Then:

1. Call a freeze moment—when everyone stops instantly!
2. Ask one child at a time, "What is the conflict?"
3. Then ask one child at a time, "Can you think of one solution for this conflict?" Come up with several possible action plans.
4. Then ask, "Is there a suggested solution you can all live with?"
5. Depending on the age and skill of the children, they may be able to move on, or they may need to role-play the solution with your coaching.

As children get more proficient at using this process, you can use it for more significant fights. Watch for times when they use this process without your coaching, and provide lots of praise!

Six Steps to Resolving a Problem

As children get older, they need conflict resolution steps that they can take in the absence of an adult. The following steps from *Knowing Me, Knowing You* are easy to remember:

1. Calm down. It is very hard to work out a conflict when you are upset and angry.
2. Talk using "I messages." When you say what you are feeling, no one gets blamed or defensive.
3. Really listen. Let the other person speak first, and really stop the chatter in your head so you can hear what the other person is saying.
4. Speak clearly and accurately. Remember all of the assertiveness techniques and pay attention to your body language.
5. Ask yourself what role you played. Think about the other person's point of view, and ask the other person to consider yours.
6. Agree to let it go and then—or later—brainstorm how to prevent this type of misunderstanding or upset from happening again.

Give your children many opportunities to define a problem, brainstorm solutions, pick one solution, develop an action plan, try it, regroup, and try another, until they successfully solve a problem or conflict. This develops their sense that they are competent and capable of resolving conflicts. Kids are far more likely to actually try solutions that they devise themselves. It is important to not be the "answer" parent, because this deprives kids of opportunities to build their own skills.

DID YOU KNOW?

Dealing with the thoughts in your own head is one of the hardest parts about being the target of a bully. The following are "Cooling Off Thoughts" offered by the Conflict Center in Denver:

- Think about what you will do when you get home.
- I can handle this!
- I don't like this, but I can get through it!
- I've heard this before, and it is not about me.
- I'm really mad now, but it won't last long.
- They are looking for a reaction, but I won't give them one.
- I am in control of what I do.

Dealing with Bullies without Getting Sucked In

Bullies test the water to see if a child is going to be a good target. Therefore, the first step is for your child not to get sucked in by the bully's attempt to engage. If a bully sees or feels a fearful response, the bullying is sure to escalate. If a child backs off or cries or takes a submissive stance, the bully has found a target. Bully-proofing your child means teaching these skills in preparation, even if there is not yet a problem.

How to "Just Ignore It"

When adults learn about kids being bullied, "Just ignore it" is the first throwaway line kids usually hear. It's a valid strategy, but it can be incredibly hard to do, especially for kids who already feel unsure or uncomfortable. Just as other life skills must be learned experientially, ignoring a bully is a learned skill. Role-play is a way for your child to prepare for negative comments and become *desensitized* to them.

> **ROLE-PLAY:** *Teasing about Physical Appearance*
> Ask your child, "What if an older kid walks by you in the lunchroom and starts teasing you about your new glasses (or braces or clothing or physical size), saying, 'Four eyes, four eyes!' What would help you to ignore that person?"
>
> **DISCUSSION:** Choose one strategy at a time, and then have your child practice ignoring you as you tease.
>
> **ACTION 1:** Talk to yourself, saying, "I knew someone was going to say that! I like my new glasses, I like being able to see, and I don't care what s/he thinks."
>
> **DISCUSSION:** Talking to yourself is one way to occupy your mind so the teasing doesn't even get in the door!
>
> **ACTION 2:** Imagine a big bubble around yourself. The words of the person teasing you hit the bubble and get stuck, but they don't get to you.
>
> **ACTION 3:** Count backward from ten, very slowly. If the bully is still there when you get to zero, start again. Keep your mind busy so you don't hear a word the bully says.
>
> **ACTION 4:** Talk to yourself, saying, "That's not true about me! That's not true about me! That's not true about me!"
>
> **PAY ATTENTION TO:** If your child starts to laugh in this process, the job is done!
>
> **ROLE-PLAY:** *Mean Comments*
> Ask, "What if the bully is using relational bullying and

saying things about you that are unkind, or telling you that your friends are saying things about you?"

DISCUSSION: Sometimes the best thing to do is to use your internal voice and just drown out what the bully is saying by giving yourself your own little talk.

ACTION 1: "I know that the bully's trying to upset me."

ACTION 2: "I know that none of those things are true about me."

ACTION 3: "I know that my friends really like me and, in fact, I'm going to find my friends right now."

Remember, ignoring is hard work, and it may not be an instant fix. If the bully is persistent, it may take a week or more for the bully to give up. Ask your child how it's going, and role-play to practice and develop new techniques for ignoring the bully. Then heap on the praise because your child is not giving in to the bully!

TALK WITH YOUR KIDS

- Think about a conflict that was really upsetting to you.
- How did you handle it?
- Did you communicate with the person about it?
- Did you consider their point of view?
- Were you blaming the other person or looking at your part in creating the conflict?
- How would you handle it differently, knowing what you know now?

Using Body Language to Ignore

Body language is another critical part of showing bullies that their behavior is irrelevant to you. Even as your child is using internal techniques to ignore a bully, the bully is also keenly aware of your child's body language. As discussed on Day 4, make sure your child's actions are reinforcing his message.

> **ROLE-PLAY:** *The Bully Shows Up*
>
> Ask, "What if a bully approaches you and there are other people nearby?"
>
> **ACTION 1:** Turn to somebody else and start a conversation with them and completely ignore the bully, even if s/he starts talking to you.
>
> **ACTION 2:** Walk over to the group and ask if you can join in.

> **ROLE-PLAY:** *"Copycat" Mean Girls*
>
> Ask, "What if a group of girls is mimicking your movements, the way you check your hair or put on your lip gloss, or the way you walk or carry your books? You never know when they will show up. Even if you ignore what they're doing, you can hear them laughing. What would you say and do?"
>
> **ACTION 1:** Practice walking straight ahead, paying attention to all of your body language: head held high, eyes forward, shoulders back, standing tall. Don't pull your books up to your chest. Don't look back at them or make faces. Use one of your thinking strategies at the same time and keep moving. Remember, this is not about you, it is about their meanness.
>
> **ACTION 2:** Identify other friends to walk with in the hall, to or from school, or at lunchtime. Practice talking to that friend even as the other girls are making their

comments. If appropriate, you could even be saying to your friend, "I know they think I care about what they are saying, but I'm glad to be friends with someone who knows what it means to be a friend. Let's just laugh them off!"

ACTION 3: Identify a glorious moment in your life to think about while you are being attacked. Other kids describe visualizing themselves as a bush with flowers and thorns. The unkind words blow through them without a ripple.

Remember, persistence is part of the game. It's not fair, it's not right, but it is the situation your child is in. Your child needs to learn not to let the unkindness of other people hurt. The ability to be resilient is powerful training for the coming years of adolescence!

Mastering the Comeback

Having a response the very first time bullying occurs can take away the bully's power. Preparing kids through role-play to respond to verbal attacks is invaluable. Bullies can be stopped by the unexpected, random, or funny comeback. As with the other skills, these only work if your child can deliver them with confidence, which comes with practice. Role-play the following strategies that seem most fitting for your child. Please also feel free to change the role-plays to use the actual insults your child is hearing. If your child is being bullied, the closer the role-plays are to reality, the more effectively they will work for your child.

1. Agreeing with the Bully

Agreeing with the bully takes the bully's power away. No matter what the bully says, agree with him or her. This appears to be a simple technique, but it takes practice and the ability to fake confidence when you're not feeling it.

ROLE-PLAY: *Nasty Comments*

Ask, "What if you encounter a bully and s/he makes nasty comments or says things about you?"

ACTION: Look right at the bully and say, "You're right," and keep moving to your classroom or wherever you were headed.

ROLE-PLAY: *Agreement*

Ask, "What if the bully says, 'Your hair is a mess.'?"

ACTION: "You are so right. I've decided to stop combing it."

ROLE-PLAY: *Going Along*

Ask, "What if the bully says 'You are so fat.'?"

ACTION: "I know, it took a long time, but I think I've got it now."

ROLE-PLAY: *More Agreement*

Ask, "What if the bully says 'You're such a retard.'?"

ACTION: "Yeah, I get a lot less homework that way."

ROLE-PLAY: *Putting the Bully Off*

Ask, "What if the bully says 'You stink.'?"

ACTION: "I know. Don't come any closer, it gets worse."

ROLE-PLAY: *Being Agreeable*

Ask, "What if the bully says, 'Your arms are like toothpicks!'?"

ACTION: "You're telling me this because. . . ?"

One young man I know became good enough at this that he began to turn the table on his nemesis, asking, "Could you explain to me why you felt you needed to say that?" The bully looked at him and walked away. In this case, other kids who had been the target of this bully took notice and gradually began to stand up to him, taking away his power to terrorize the lunchroom.

2. Permission to Keep It Up

Permission to keep it up also works to let a bully know you don't care.

> **ROLE-PLAY: *Thank You***
> Ask, "What if the bully says 'You're Special Ed, get away from our table.'?"
> **ACTION:** "Thanks, I'm glad you know I'm here."

> **ROLE-PLAY: *Look Like a Girl***
> Ask, "What if the bully says, 'You look like a girl.'?"
> **ACTION:** "Thanks for noticing."

> **ROLE-PLAY: *You Noticed***
> Ask, "What if the bully says 'You've worn that outfit three times this week—what a loser.'?"
> **ACTION:** "You noticed! You're making my day."

3. Countering the Insult

Countering the insult also works to let the bully know that you are not intimidated and can hold your own.

> **ROLE-PLAY: *Pay Extra***
> Ask, "What if the bully says, 'Don't go near him; he has cooties.'?"
> **ACTION:** "Hey, you have to pay extra to get those."

> **ROLE-PLAY: *Who Cares?***
> Ask, "What if the bully says, 'You can't do anything right—what a loser you are.'?"

ACTION: "You're confusing me with someone who cares."

4. The Stare-Down

A bully glaring menacingly at your child is another form of intimidation. Have your child stare back.

> **ROLE-PLAY:** *Stare Down*
> Practice walking toward your child staring the whole time. Your child should be able to stare equally until you pass one another. Talk about how this feels. Your child's goal is to be able to hold his head up and make eye contact without avoiding the bully's glare.

5. Shrug It Off

Body language that says "Whatever" can be very effective.

> **ROLE-PLAY:** *Whatever*
> Have your child practice shrugging her shoulders, with her hands pointed up to the ceiling, saying, "Whatever" with her words and body, and rolling her eyes.

6. Drawing Attention to the Bully

Drawing attention to the bully can also work. Change the situation so observers wonder what the bully is doing. This can stop bullies in their tracks. This, too, has to be done with confidence, so practice is a must.

> **ROLE-PLAY:** *Whispered Insults*
> Ask, "What if the bully gets close to you to whisper an insult?"
> **ACTION:** Loudly say, "Hey, get your hands off me!"

ROLE-PLAY: *You Think What?*

Ask, "What if the bully says, 'You're so ugly.'?"

ACTION: Loudly say, "You think what?"

ROLE-PLAY: *Pushing*

Ask, "What if the bully pushes you into the locker?"

ACTION: Loudly say, "Hey, keep your hands to yourself!"

When a Bully Escalates

Fighting with a bully is a bad idea. Bullies tend to pick on kids who are not as strong, aggressive, or confident as they are. Physical responses to bullies are likely to end up with kids getting hurt, and a defeat certainly will not contribute to ending the bullying or boosting the targeted child's self-confidence.

When a bully escalates beyond verbal insults, all the skills your child has been learning need to come together. When children are confronted by a bully, the one thing they can control is how they respond to that situation. At that moment, your child is pulling together all the things you have worked on: communication, assertiveness, self-confidence, body language, problem solving, and self-reliance. While you may have practiced most of these in the process of the role-playing and brainstorming in the book, actually pulling them together in the context of a problem your child is experiencing will make them real and applicable skills.

Bullies can come to control a child's every waking thought and action. Following are some strategies your child might want to practice in preparation for avoiding or dealing with the next confrontation with a bully. It is not right that your child should have to prepare for all of these possibilities, or that your child should be thinking about the bully rather than school or play or other friends. But remember, the reality of the situation is that most bullying occurs out of the sight of adults. Your child has to have the skills to stand up for him- or herself when the bully shows up.

At the same time, the school and the community have a responsibility to provide a safe environment, free of harassment, for all kids. So, even as your child is developing these coping strategies, you should be talking to the adults surrounding the situation and asking for their help to stop the bullying.

Strategies for dealing with an escalating bully:

- Prevention is the best practice. Make sure that you're not alone with the bully in the bathroom, an empty classroom, a long hallway, a locker room, or an isolated part of the playground.
- Make sure you have someone to hang out with when you're on the playground.
- If you're walking to or from school, hanging out during lunchtime, or waiting for the bus, be sure you're with someone. If you're with other people, you're less vulnerable to all kinds of potentially threatening situations.
- If the bully bumps into you in the hall, or pushes you, or trips you, or knocks your books out of your hands, look at the bully and say, "Excuse me," pick up your things, and move on. It can be hard not to escalate the situation, but the bully is looking for you to do exactly that. By saying "excuse me" and moving on, you deny the bully the reaction s/he was trying to get and s/he's less likely to bother you again.
- If a bully demands that you hand over your money or something that belongs to you, you have to make a decision in that moment. Is it safe to just ignore the bully and walk away, or is it better to give your lunch money to the bully and then immediately tell your classroom teacher or another adult? If you feel safe enough

to say "no" and walk away, do that. If you feel threatened, it is time to get an adult involved anyway, so give up the money and get to an adult.

- Finally, remind yourself that fighting is not an option. Getting into a physical altercation with a bully is a sure way to get yourself kicked out of school, to get yourself hurt, or to be blamed for having started it, when in fact it was the bully who started it. If you are physically assaulted, get out of the situation and get help from an adult. Do not listen to your fear that it will get worse or your idea that you can avoid the bully in the future—the situation is more than you should try to handle by yourself.

- Even as you are using these strategies, keep your parents and teachers informed. This is not whining or tattling. It is smart to bring all the resources you have to addressing this problem. Trying to handle an escalating bully on your own is not smart or necessary.

Children who successfully learn to handle a bully have a giant surge in their self-confidence and self-esteem, knowing they can rely on their own resources. This is the reason it is so important not to jump right in and rescue your children when they are being bullied. I know how painful it is to watch a child work to develop these skills, but the process of trying and failing and trying again and experiencing success is the most powerful way for kids to master the ability to stand up for themselves, and eventually for others.

DAY 7: SUMMING IT UP

Conflict is a part of life; we will never be without it. But conflict is also a learning opportunity, a chance for kids to develop critical skills. The steps in conflict resolution are:

- Focus on the solution, not on who is at fault.
- Define the conflict.
- Practice generating ideas to resolve the conflict.
- Learn to recognize the feelings generated by the conflict.
- Identify their reactions to others involved.
- Choose an option to resolve the conflict.

Actually applying these skills to bullying situations can take many forms. One of the objectives is to not get sucked into the bully's game. This is accomplished most successfully by using role-play to practice in advance. Techniques include:

- Learn to ignore it; desensitize.
- Master the comeback; learn a few scripted lines that can be used in tense or intimidating situations.
- Body language says volumes—learn to use it.

If there is already a bullying problem, give kids avoidance or safety strategies they can use while adults are trying to help solve the problem.

Being a Good Friend

Q: *"I was recently contacted by a mother who told me how devastated her daughter, age thirteen, was because she had been excluded from the overnight for my daughter's birthday. I tried to smooth it over by telling her that we didn't have room to invite everyone. She was persistent and went into a whole list of unkind things that my daughter had said in phone messages and e-mail. I recognized them because my daughter had said the same things at home, but I never dreamed she would say them to the girl directly. I talked to my daughter, and she said even more dreadful things about this girl and showed no remorse at all! I know this is unacceptable behavior, but I can't force her to like the girl. What is the appropriate way to handle this situation?"*
—Frannie M., *parent of thirteen-year-old*

SHERRYLL SAYS: *"This is where being able to relate to the feelings of someone else comes into play. Through discussion, see if you can get your daughter connected to what it feels like to have people say unkind things. If necessary, role-play saying mean things to her to see if you can get her to experience how it feels to be the target of mean words and acts. She is at an age where friends come and go; she might find herself the target of similar unkind behavior in the future. It is also appropriate to set some boundaries, to identify her behavior as what it is: bullying. It is important to say that bullying is not acceptable, and she cannot do it. She can have any thoughts she wants, but she doesn't have the right to communicate them with the intention or outcome of hurting others."*

Friendship is one of the most powerful ways for your child to avoid being a bully or a target. Children who know how to be kind, who have at least one good friend, and who know how to move success-fully in and out of peer groups have the best chance of avoiding the bully trap. I believe we need to teach friendship skills directly. Most kids don't naturally know how to be friends, much less how to be a good friend.

Being a friend starts with all those skills we've talked about that build a positive sense of self. Confidence, resiliency, good communication skills, and the ability to read social cues are all elements of your child's personal toolbox. They are what enable your child not to internalize the slights that occur in friendships or to wonder if she did something to deserve this treatment. A child with high self-esteem and good skills knows—from the inside out—that "It is not about me."

TEN QUICK TIPS FOR MAKING NEW FRIENDS!

1. Think about what kind of people you like. What are your interests? Do you want to hang out with people interested in what you are interested in, or do you want to try out new things?

2. Talk to people in a friendly and polite way. Be inter-ested in what other people have to say. Ask questions about what they are interested in.

3. Smile! People like being around happy people. Com-plaining about everything drives people away. Being a gossip or passing on rumors makes people think you will start rumors about them, and they will stay away from you.

4. Be positive! People who badmouth other people, who

are sarcastic and condescending, drive other people away. The old adage, "If you can't say something nice, don't say anything at all" applies here.

5. Build up your confidence. "Fake it till you make it!" Stand up, look people in the eye, and listen carefully. Try to enjoy whatever you are doing.

6. Ask questions. Show your interest in what others have to say. Share your ideas in such a way that the conversation continues.

7. Be an active listener. Empathize with others.

8. Call your friends and see how they're doing. Let them know if you like being their friend.

9. Laugh! Be good company and have a good time. Being with friends and new people should be fun.

10. Be yourself. Share your interests and ideas. If you have a talent, let it show!

Nine Friendship Skills

The following are nine essential friendship skills that will help your child make new friends, maintain existing friendships, and overcome common problems like bossiness, gossip, and taking sides. You can practice these skills through role-play scenarios.

1. Learn How to Join a Group
A critical skill for children is learning how to invite themselves into a group. Simple sentences like, "Can I play this game with you?" make a big difference. If you see your child hanging at the edge of a group, suggest s/he go up and say, "This looks like fun, can I work on that with you?" This is another area where the ability to read social cues is so important. Children need to be able to accurately read the way others are responding to them.

Another way to gradually become friends with a new group of kids is to get to know one child in the group a little better. You can suggest, and then role-play with your child, asking a child to come over after school or go to a movie or play a game on the playground. Breaking the ice is always the hardest part, and your coaching will enable your child to develop this as a real skill.

> **ROLE-PLAY:** *Welcoming Party*
> Say, "I'm going to have a party so we can meet all the kids in your class and some of their parents. I'd like you to invite each of the kids to come. What do you think you would say?"
> **ACTION 1:** "We just moved here and I'm having a party for everyone in the class. Here's the invitation. I hope you can come."
> **DISCUSSION:** Check your child's body language, tone of voice, and eye contact. Practice so it is easy and your child's demeanor is inviting.

If your child is starting a new school, find out what clubs or groups exist that fit with your child's interests. Have a welcoming party for your family and invite all the kids in your child's class. Host a picnic with families in your neighborhood. Set up a lemonade stand or Girl Scout cookie stand in front of your house. Getting started is the hardest part. Once your child has a few neighborhood friends, others usually follow.

Children who do not pick up on social cues need to be taught quite explicitly about verbal and nonverbal cues. The earlier chapter on communication and all the elements of nonverbal communication is particularly important for them. Without these skills, they may not realize when they are being made fun of, or how to gain entry in to a group that is genuine rather than exploitive. They need to become as skilled as possible in the give and take of relating to peers, the rules of appropriate behavior, friendship, and being part of a group.

2. Keep Your Agreements

Being trustworthy is perhaps the greatest asset for building lifelong friendships. This is a skill to teach your children from kindergarten on. Let kids know that:

- When you promise to keep a friend's secret, sharing it with "just one person" is not all right, unless someone's safety is at stake.
- Getting a better offer is not a reason to blow off a friend you've already made plans with.
- When you say you'll do something for another person, follow through. Changing your mind is not sufficient reason to break a commitment.

Kids who can be counted on to be there, who listen, who stand up for others, who speak up in the face of thoughtless or unkind behavior are the kinds of kids who make and keep good friends.

ROLE-PLAY: *Should You Cancel on a Friend?*
Ask your child, "What if you promised your friend that you would spend the night at his house, and then someone else calls and asks you to go to a Laser Tag party? You'd rather do that. What are you going to say and do?"
ACTION 1: "I'm not going to spend the night. I'll tell him I'd rather go to Laser Tag."
DISCUSSION: Unless his friend can go too, there is no way out of this that won't be hurtful. Your child needs to keep his agreement, and you need to resist the urge to

create an excuse that will rescue him from his ethical problem. This is easier said than done!

ACTION 2: "I'd really love to go to Laser Tag, but I've made other plans."

DISCUSSION: Talk about this option honestly. It doesn't always feel good to be ethical. Discuss why it is important nevertheless.

ROLE-PLAY: *A Friend Lies*

Ask, "What if a friend had agreed to spend the night over here, but he calls and says he is sick? Later on, you find out that he went to a Laser Tag party instead. What would you say or do?"

ACTION 1: "I can't believe you lied to me about coming over!"

DISCUSSION: Although your child is feeling hurt and angry about what his friend has done, talk about whether or not this would make matters worse.

ACTION 2: "I found out that you went to the Laser Tag party. It would have been okay to tell me you had a better invitation."

DISCUSSION: This response puts what happened on the table and gives the friend permission to be more honest in the relationship.

3. Be an Active Listener

A key element of being a good friend is listening—just listening. We all have opinions about things our friends say and do. We may even have advice. But sometimes our friends don't want to hear it; they just want to be heard. Alert your child to the value of just listening, of repeating back what s/he's heard, and of empathizing rather than automatically jumping in to do something.

For example, say your child's friend is crushed because she didn't make the debate team. Speaking back her feelings and empathizing might sound like this, "I know you're really disappointed that you didn't make the team." If your child's friend has just heard about an insult from a peer, your child has a choice to escalate the situation or to say, "You're really angry about what he said; I can hear it in your voice."

> **ROLE-PLAY: *Left Out***
> Ask, "What if your friend tells you that she didn't get invited to go to a skating party with a group of other first graders. You didn't get invited either, but you are not as upset about it as she is. What could you do to help her feel better?
> **ACTION 1:** "I'd tell her it wouldn't have been any fun anyway."
> **DISCUSSION:** Telling her it doesn't matter or that you don't like those kids anyway might be very satisfying, but your friend might just want you to be sympathetic. Help your child to focus on the feelings rather than on what the other children did.
> **ACTION 2:** "I know that you were really hoping to go. You must be disappointed. Is there something we could do together?"
> **DISCUSSION:** Talk about the value of empathy and reflecting what your child's friend is feeling.

We all appreciate being heard. As parents, we often want to jump in and fix everything or speak up to defend our children. But, when children feel heard and understood, it is easier for them to let go of some of what they are feeling and develop an action plan to solve their own problems.

ROLE-PLAY: *Listen!*

Ask, "What if you were really angry with the other boys for breaking your model airplane? They were careless and didn't listen when you told them to be careful. You are trying to make your friend understand how angry you are, and he just keeps telling you, 'Get over it. It's broken!'"

ACTION 1: "Stop telling me it's broken! I know it's broken, that's why I'm so mad!"

DISCUSSION: Sometimes we just want other people to acknowledge our upset, and they try to get us to forget it, or forgive, or let go of it. But what if you're not ready to let go of it, and you want your friend to be more sympathetic. What could you say?

ACTION 2: "I know it's broken! I just want you to listen and understand how angry I am about it. Then I can get over it!"

4. Don't Say Everything You Think

Being judgmental is a trait that loses its charm quickly. We all have opinions, but being a friend sometimes means keeping them to yourself. One of the fastest ways to make friends mad is to tell them what they should or shouldn't have done. "You shouldn't have let him read your diary." "You shouldn't have lied to your mother. You know she always finds out." We are all our own worst critic, so your friends probably already know what they did wrong, and they don't want to hear it again from you. Either hold your tongue or ask a question such as, "What are you going to do about it now?" Focus on the forward action, not the mistake, if you want to help your friend move on.

On the other hand, sometimes friends get involved in really stupid or unsafe activities. This might be a time when being a friend means asking questions about the choices a friend is making, questions that are designed to get your friend to reconsider.

ROLE-PLAY: *Hair Color*

Ask, "What if your best friend asks you if her newly colored hair is too red?"

ACTION 1: "I think it is a little too bright."

DISCUSSION: Even if you think it is, should you say so? Do you think that might make her feel worse?

ACTION 2: "Aren't you happy with it?"

DISCUSSION: Responding to the concern your friend is expressing might be better than offering an opinion she didn't want to hear.

DID YOU KNOW?

Good friends stick with you through whatever is going on. www.girlshealth.gov provides these "7 Ways to know if your friends really care about you":

- They are interested in your well-being, and not in what you might give them or do for them.
- They listen and care about what you have to say.
- They are happy for you when you do well.
- They say they are sorry when they make a mistake.
- They don't expect you to be perfect.
- They give you advice in a caring way.
- They respect your privacy.

5. Don't Participate in Gossip and Rumors

Gossip and rumors are the domain of girls. They are rampant, vicious, and designed to hurt. This activity reaches its height in middle school and doesn't diminish until after high school. One of the patterns is retaliatory gossip. "You said something about me, so I'll say something about you." The opportunity for parents to actively confront rumors and gossip is in the elementary-school years, before they are completely entrenched.

Part of teaching our children not to gossip includes being conscious of our own level of tolerance for gossip. Do we do it ourselves? How do we respond when others include us in their gossip? How do we handle it when we hear that others have gossiped about us? Children learn from how we behave, and so we need to be vigilant about what messages come and go in our home.

Most parents become aware of the power of gossip and rumors when their own daughter learns that she is the object of a rumor, and they are suddenly confronted with how painful and heart-breaking it is. The power of all the skills we have talked about so far is needed to deal with this. A child who is the object of gossip and rumors needs to confront the problem clearly and assertively, without tears or rage. You will need to role-play (perhaps many times!) a conversation with her friends or the person responsible for the rumor, saying, "That is not true about me, and I want you to stop telling lies about me." This takes a lot of courage and confidence. It is also one of the best ways to learn not to engage in subsequent rumors and gossip.

> **ROLE-PLAY:** *Instant Messaging Gossip*
> Ask, "What if your friends have taken a piece of infor-
> mation about another girl in school and are spreading
> it around through instant messaging, voice mail, and
> notes at school? You know what they are saying is true.
> At the same time, you know that it is hurtful to the girl
> and her ability to even go to school. What would you
> say and do?"
> **ACTION 1:** Send an e-mail to everyone involved, saying,
>   "This needs to stop. She's already in enough trouble
>   without us making her life miserable."
> **DISCUSSION:** Would it cost your child anything to take

this bold step? What would be the possible negative fallout? What would be the possible positive results? How do you decide to take the risk?

ROLE-PLAY: *Spreading Rumors*
Ask, "What if your friend is spreading rumors about you and you find out? What would you say and do?"

ACTION 1: "I know you are part of spreading this rumor. As a friend, I'm asking you to not only stop but to tell people this isn't true."

ACTION 2: "I don't understand what is happening here. What could you do to help stop this rumor about me?"

DISCUSSION: It takes enormous courage to confront situations like this. Role-play! Practice is essential to build the confidence to have this discussion. Talk about the risks and potential benefits of having this discussion with a friend.

TALK WITH YOUR KIDS

- Have you ever been excluded from a party or sleepover? How did you feel?
- Have you ever excluded other people? How did they act when they found out they were excluded? Did you feel bad about what you had done? What did you do?
- Have you ever found out that people are gossiping about you? How did you feel? What did you do?
- Have you ever gossiped about someone else? How did that feel? Did the other person find out? What did she do? How did you feel then?
- Did you ever have a friend who just stopped talking to you or playing with you? How did you feel? What

did you do? Have you ever done that to one of your
friends? Why? Did you talk to your friend about it, or
just exclude her?

■ What are the things that you value most in your
friends?

■ What do you think your friends like most about
you?

6. Don't Pit Your Friends against One Another

Just as gossip and rumors about kids outside your social circle are
damaging, "nattering" or "dissing" other kids within your circle
of friends is deadly. This often happens as a part of establishing or
trying to change the pecking order of a group. As one girl becomes
the center of attention in a group, another may try to take her place
by talking her down to the others. This is deadly because it always
comes back around to where it started.

If you hear your child engage in conversations or actions that
threaten the stability of a group of friends, talk openly about what
is going on openly. Likewise, if your child is the victim of shifting
allegiances, talk about that as well. Often, bringing the dynamic
into the open stops it. At the same time, it gives young people
insight into what is happening, so they can make an informed
choice about their own behavior and that of others.

7. Share Power and Control

Sharing power and control means learning to be in charge sometimes and then to let others be in charge. It means listening as
much as you talk. It includes valuing the ideas of others and sharing the spotlight. Bossy children often have good social skills,
but their use of language makes it difficult for them to integrate
into a group.

The fastest way to shift this problem is to help your children change their language. Notice how these paired statements, things parents commonly say, feel very different:

- "Don't go out until you show me your homework." vs. "Please let me take a look at your homework before you go out."
- "You have to go to bed now." vs. "I'd like for you to go to bed now so you'll be full of energy for our trip tomorrow."
- "You need to call your coach about missing last night's game." vs. "Do you want to give your coach a call? I'm sure he's wondering where you were last night."

Likewise, children need to learn to be less demanding. They need to say, "Mom, would you make me a glass of chocolate milk?" rather than, "Mom, I want some chocolate milk." When your child is bossy, be explicit in naming your reaction. For example, "I don't want to go shopping with you when you are demanding. Please try asking me in another way." If your child doesn't have the skills to ask more appropriately, model what you are looking for: "Mom, I'd like something new to wear to the party tomorrow. Would you have time to take me shopping today?"

Changing a child's pattern of speaking takes many repetitions. Keep at it—the payoff will be tremendous. Many friendships are lost because of an imbalance of power and pure lack of consideration for the other person. Practice with role-play and follow-up discussion to build your child's insight about relationships.

ROLE-PLAY: *Weekend Trip*
Ask, "What if you're angry because your friend doesn't want to go to the skate park with you this weekend?"
ACTION 1: "I'm going to go to the skate park whether you want to or not!"
DISCUSSION: Ask your child if this approach will help or make things worse for the relationship. Practice other

ways of presenting the dilemma, including a proposal
that will share the decision making.

ACTION 2: "I want to go to the skate park, and you want
to play Xbox. Can we do one on Saturday and one
on Sunday?"

8. Presume Good Intentions

*My niece spent weeks working on a scrapbook for my oldest daughter.
It was pretty spectacular. My younger daughter was jealous and began
to treat her cousin very badly. When I finally got to the bottom of it,
she said she felt really left out. Then it turned out that my niece was
making one for her as well. This was such a great lesson. My younger
daughter spent weeks thinking that her cousin liked her sister more.
This wasn't the case at all, and we were able to really talk about how
assumptions can get you in trouble!*

—Jill S., *mother of ten- and twelve-year-olds*

Assuming that you know what someone else thinks or believes is
almost always a mistake. Assumptions are the basis for many of
the misunderstandings and disagreements that happen between
close friends. When your children are upset about something
that they think or believe has happened, sit down with them to
discuss the problem and determine a way to get the facts! Making
a clear distinction between what happened and any perceptions
about what happened is critical. I have participated in so many
problem-solving sessions in which kids have talked about the
"intentions" of their friends with absolutely no real information
about anyone's intention.

Teach your children to first "presume good intentions." Most
kids don't spend their time trying to figure out how to hurt their
friends. Misunderstandings look different in the light of presuming good intentions than they do when we assume that someone
meant to hurt our feelings. Presuming good intentions also

changes the nature of the response and leaves room for clarifying rather than escalating a situation.

> **ROLE-PLAY:** *Hurt Feelings*
> Ask, "What if your friend said something that hurt your feelings, and you feel that she did it on purpose? What might you say or do?"
>
> **ACTION 1:** "I would tell her exactly how I feel about what she did."
>
> **DISCUSSION:** Is there another way of looking at what happened? How could you let her know how you feel about what happened without making her angry or making the situation worse?
>
> **ACTION 2:** "I know you probably didn't mean to hurt my feelings, but I was really upset by what you said."
>
> **DISCUSSION:** Your friend might apologize and then you can both move on. But what if your friend gets defensive right away, saying, "Well, aren't you the sensitive one!"
>
> **ACTION 3:** You can choose to escalate the fight or just let it go, saying, "I know, I can be really thin-skinned. I know you didn't mean to hurt me. I just wanted to tell you so I can let go of it."

Sometimes this type of exploration will uncover an actual intention to hurt someone's feelings. You might hear a statement like, "She hurt my feelings, so I made sure she knows what that feels like!" When this happens, deal with it directly. Sit down with both girls and discuss how it feels to be deliberately hurtful, how it hurts relationships, and how it makes it that much harder to trust each other and remain friends. Develop a plan for communicating about future disputes or hurt feelings, discuss how to listen to each other rather than planning the next defensive remark, and then role-play. Learning to speak up when your feelings have been hurt or when you feel slighted is not easy and takes practice.

WHAT IS CONFLICT RESOLUTION?

Conflict resolution is a way to work through and resolve disputes, disagreements, or misunderstandings. Most conflict resolution programs follow a series of steps that include:

1. **Setting ground rules**. Agree to work together and set rules such as no name-calling, blaming, yelling, or interrupting.
2. **Listening.** Let each person describe his or her point of view without interruption. The point is to understand what a person wants and why she wants it.
3. **Finding common interests**. Establish facts and issues that everyone can agree on, and determine what is important to each person.
4. **Brainstorming possible solutions to the problem**. List all options without judging them or feeling that they must be carried out. Try to think of solutions where everyone gains something.
5. **Discussing each person's view of the proposed solutions**. Negotiate and try to reach a compromise that is acceptable to everyone involved.
6. **Reaching an agreement**. Each person should state his or her interpretation of the agreement. Try writing the agreement down and checking back at a later time to see how it is working.

From: www.safeyouth.org

9. Let Go of Past Hurts

Learning to let go of the past is a lifelong challenge for most of us. Look for opportunities to coach your child on letting go of past offenses, on allowing people to change, on not using events to pit people against one another.

> **ROLE-PLAY:** *Past Incident*
> Ask, "What if a friend of yours keeps bringing up an incident that happened last summer? You've talked about it lots of times, and she keeps coming back to it. It is making it hard to be her friend. What could you say or do to put an end to it?"
>
> **ACTION:** "We've talked about that and I apologized. Now let's put an end to it and agree to not bring it up again."
>
> **PAY ATTENTION TO:** Tone of voice—no whining or being meek. Practice this role-play to achieve a clear and assertive presentation.
>
> **ROLE-PLAY:** *Complaints*
> Ask, "What if you're sitting around with a group of friends. They start complaining for the umpteenth time about another friend of yours and something s/he did that they didn't like. What could you say and do to stop their constant criticizing?"
>
> **ACTION:** "Will you guys cut it out? We've all done stupid stuff. Let's move past this!"
>
> **PAY ATTENTION TO:** Tone of voice and presentation. The goal is to be clear but not too aggressive. Practice this role-play to achieve a clear and assertive presentation.

Trevor Romain offers these ten wonderfully simple tips for keeping friends in his book *Cliques, Phonies, & Other Baloney:*

1. Show them kindness and respect.
2. Stick up for them.
3. Be supportive when your friends need help or advice.
4. Tell the truth (but be kind about it).
5. If you hurt a friend, say you're sorry.
6. If a friend hurts you and apologizes, accept the apology.
7. If you make a promise, keep it.
8. Put some effort into your friendships: so your friends don't feel neglected.
9. Don't try to change your friends—accept them the way they are.
10. Treat your friends the way you want them to treat you.

DAY 8: SUMMING IT UP

Friendships come and go with great pain for most young people. As kids grow, learning to navigate friendships is central to developing relationship skills that will carry them through their lives. Key elements include:

1. Be positive, share your ideas and interests; learn how to join a group.
2. Be someone your friends can count on. Keep your agreements.
3. Be interested; be an active listener.
4. Don't say everything you think; curb your judgments and opinions.
5. Don't participate in gossip and rumors.
6. Don't pit your friends against one another, it always comes back around.
7. Learn to share power and control—don't be too bossy or too weak.
8. Presume good intentions; most miscommunications aren't intended to be mean.
9. Be a good listener; learn to really hear what people want to say.
10. Let go of past hurts; allow people to learn and change.

Staying Safe Online: Preventing Cyber-Bullying

Q: *"My son was dating a girl who called him on his cell phone day and night. She sent dozens of text messages every day. She filled his e-mail box with endless diatribes about his failure to spend enough time with her. My son got pretty tired of it and broke up with her, but the messages kept coming. Then her new boyfriend got into the act, and the messages got more explicit and threatening. My son's mood changed, he refused to go out at night, and he wouldn't talk about what was going on. So I did something I thought I would never do. While he was asleep I checked his phone and his e-mail and found the messages. I told him in the morning that I knew what was happening. He was profoundly relieved. We got a restraining order and, maybe more importantly, had a much-needed conversation about asking for help when you're in over your head!"*

—Nancy E., *parent of fourteen-year-old*

SHERRYLL SAYS: *"You did exactly the right thing! While we all wish that our kids would be forthcoming, they often aren't. If you sense that something is wrong and your child isn't talking, you need to take whatever steps you feel are necessary to intervene and protect your child. This is increasingly true as more and more strangers have access to children through electronic media. You not only addressed the problem, you taught your son an important lesson about the need to ask for help when you can't solve a problem by yourself."*

Technology is moving faster than most parents, but our kids are having no problem keeping up. The many ways kids connect via technology—like instant messaging, text messaging, and posting comments on personal Web pages—have changed the landscape for interpersonal communication and extended the reach of bullies. Today the focus is on establishing or clarifying electronic safety, understanding electronic bullying, and developing strategies to avoid this problem area.

DID YOU KNOW?

- A 2006 survey found that 9 percent of young Internet users said they were harassed online in the past year.
- Six percent said someone was bothering or harassing them online, and 3 percent said someone had posted or sent messages about them for other people to see.
- Three percent described an incident of distressing online harassment that left them feeling "very or extremely upset or afraid."
- The targets were 58 percent girls and 42 percent boys.
- Girls were more likely than boys to experience distressing harassment (68 percent compared to 32 percent).
- The majority of harassment episodes (72 percent) happened to teenagers aged fourteen to seventeen.
- 42 percent of kids have been bullied while online. One in four has had it happen more than once.
- Thirty-five percent of kids have been threatened online. Nearly one in five has had it happen more than once.

- Twenty-one percent of kids have received mean or threatening e-mail or other messages.
- Fifty-eight percent of kids admit someone has said mean or hurtful things to them online. More than four out of ten say it has happened more than once.

Cyber-Communication 101

The world of electronics and the availability of the Internet are expanding rapidly. Your children can access the Internet from the computer, cell phones, PDAs, and portable media players such as iPods. Their access to appropriate and inappropriate materials is virtually unlimited, and the importance of understanding how to navigate the Internet, how to stay out of trouble, and how to communicate with people safely is paramount. First a few definitions:

1. **Blog** stands for web log. A blog is basically a journal that is available on the Internet. The activity of updating a blog is *blogging*, and someone who keeps a blog is a *blogger*. Blogs are updated frequently, and personal blogs usually have a pretty small audience base. The range and power of blogs are rapidly shifting. Blogs are increasingly a way to network socially, as well as a way to bring the public into the arena of investigative reporting and social accountability.

2. A **chatroom** is an Internet site where talk (chat) is ongoing among groups (rooms) of people on the Internet. There is usually more than one conversation going on simultaneously, which is why they are called chatrooms. Many chatrooms are monitored for unacceptable, offensive, racist, violent, and sexual content, but many are not. There is often a steady stream of people entering and leaving. Whether you are in

another person's chatroom, or one you've created yourself, you are generally free to invite others online to join. The most important thing to remember is that anyone can view profiles and conversations without their presence being known.

3. **Instant messaging** differs from e-mail because it allows people to communicate with one another over a network, such as Yahoo! or MSN Messenger, in relative privacy. Instant messaging does not leave a historical record that is easily available on the computer to be checked later, as an e-mail does. Kids can add friends to a contact list or buddy list by entering their e-mail address or messenger ID. If they are online, their name will be listed as available for chat. Clicking on their name will activate a chat window with space to write to the other person, as well as read their reply.

4. **Text messaging** through cell phones and PDAs is very common among young people. Most kids do not think about erasing what they have sent or received. This includes text, photos, and video.

5. **Social networking sites** allow people to gather online. Anyone can post a personal profile, which often includes topics of interest, personal photographs, art, music, location, age, gender, and the like.

6. **Virtual worlds and multiplayer online games** are services that make it possible to meet and interact with other people in a virtual world—which looks somewhat like reality. This can range from sites where people from all over the world join to play the same game to more reality-based sites like Sims.

MySpace

MySpace is currently one of the largest of the social networks. It is an online community that allows people to keep up with their friends and to meet new people as well. As www.techterm.org describes MySpace, anyone fourteen years old and up can create an account at no cost. Once you sign up, you can customize your profile by adding information about yourself, listing your interests, hobbies, and educational background, and uploading photos of yourself and your friends. You can also create your own blog for others to read.

Once you have created a profile on MySpace, you can search or browse other users' profiles. If you want to add someone as a friend, just click the "Add to Friends" link on that person's profile page. If the person approves your "friend request," he or she will be added to your list of friends. Some users have only a few friends, while others have several thousand. You can send a private message to a user by clicking the "Send Message" link or post a comment on his or her page by clicking "Add Comment." Comments can be seen by all visitors to that person's profile, so be careful what you post!

The "friends" concept is the heart and soul of MySpace. By building a list of friends, you have your own network of people readily accessible from your profile page. When you click on a friend's image, you can view their profile and all their friends. This makes it easy to meet friends of friends, and so on. The number of people you can meet on MySpace is practically endless, which may be a part of the reason there are so many "MySpace addicts" out there.

Internet Safety 101

From the time children begin using technology, whether computers or cell phones, there are a few basic rules that need to be discussed and enforced. These rules not only help to protect children from exploitation, they lay the groundwork for prevention of bullying. They establish a basis for communication about what happens on the Internet and for asking for help if they are being bullied or harassed electronically. The rules also provide a context for talking about bullying behaviors and why they are unkind, unacceptable, and often illegal.

1. Keep equipment accessible to the entire family. Kids don't need computers in their rooms or in the basement where you can't readily see what is going on. Walk by often and take a look at what they are doing. Ask questions. If they have a home page on one of the social sites such as MySpace, ask them to show it to you. *This is the single most important thing you can do to protect your young children and teenagers from online problems.*

2. Discuss all aspects of the technology with your children. This includes what types of sites are appropriate and are not. Be very clear that they are not to open e-mails from people they do not know and that they should not click through to unknown sites just because they show up in an e-mail or a pop-up. The balance between curiosity and following the rules is really hard for kids with computers, and parental diligence is important.

3. Never allow your children to have passwords on their computers that you do not know.

4. Set rules regarding forms, inquiries, and questionnaires. Children should never provide personal information online. If they want to order something or respond to an inquiry, they need to ask for your approval and assistance every time.

5. Discuss who gets your child's cell phone number and

the circumstances under which it can be given out. Set guidelines for text messaging and let them know that all text messages and Internet messages leave a record that is readily available. Let them know that you expect them to be respectful in their electronic communications, that harassing others is not permitted.

6. Be clear with them that they should come to you immediately with upsetting messages or invitations to get together with someone they have met online. Let them know that they will not be in trouble and that they should not erase these messages before you see them. Remind them that it isn't possible to know the age, sex, or intentions of people on the other side of electronic communication. It is better to ask an adult for help than to take a risk.

7. Be open with teens about what's out there, and encourage them to come to you if they encounter an uncomfortable situation. Family discussions about Internet safety will pay off as the technology continues to enable anonymous communication.

8. Show an interest in your teen's blog or Web site. Run a search periodically of your child's name, phone number, and address. You may find social networking postings that give you an opportunity to have further discussions.

9. It has been my experience that, as they get older, young people often want to meet in person with friends they have met on local chat sites. Since they are quite capable of doing this on their own, my rule is that they go with you to meet the new person at that person's home, or another location with the other person's parent present.

SAFE BLOGGING TIPS FOR TEENS

- **Be as anonymous as possible.** Avoid postings that could enable a stranger to locate you. That includes your last name, the name of your school, sports teams, the town you live in, and where you hang out.

- **Protect your info.** Check to see if your service has a "friends" list that allows you to control who can visit your profile or blog. If so, allow only people you know and trust. If you don't use privacy features, anyone can see your info.

- **Avoid in-person meetings.** Don't get together with someone you "meet" in a profile or blog unless you are certain of that person's actual identity. Although it's still not risk-free, if you do meet the person, arrange the meeting in a public place and bring some friends—or even better, your parents.

- **Photos: think before posting.** What's uploaded to the 'Net can be downloaded by anyone and passed around or posted online pretty much forever. Avoid posting photos that allow people to identify you (for example, when they're searching for your high school), especially sexually suggestive images. Before uploading a photo, think about how you'd feel if it were seen by a parent/grandparent, college admissions counselor, or future employer.

- **Check comments regularly.** If you allow them on your profile or blog, check them often. Don't respond to mean or embarrassing comments. Delete them and, if possible, block offensive people from commenting further.

- **Be honest about your age.** Membership rules are there to protect people. If you are too young to sign up, do not attempt to lie about your age. Talk with your friends or parents about alternative sites that may be appropriate for you.

© 2006 www.BlogSafety.com

Electronic Bullies

Q: *"My son was very engaged on the computer last evening. It was clear to me that he was in a chat room of some sort, and I kept walking by to keep an eye on things. Then the laughter changed, and I knew something was up. I walked over and saw that he had typed in the name and phone number of a girl in his class. He was pretending to be her in a conversation with an older guy. I hit the roof, got on the chat myself, and told the older guy that I would be turning his communication over to the police, at which point he and all my sons' friends quickly exited the site. I really thought my son knew better. We'd had all the safety conversations! Now my question is whether or not I should notify the girl's family."*

—Peggy W., *mother of thirteen-year-old*

SHERRYLL SAYS: *"Absolutely! Your son has put her in jeopardy. Her family has to know what happened, so they can talk to her about her own safety should this man call. Your son should also be required to write a letter of apology to her and her family. I also think the parents of the other kids involved in this chatroom behavior should be notified, so they, too, can have conversations with their children. I am certain that this is not the first time your son and his friends have done this kind of thing, and it needs to be stopped now!"*

Computers, cell phones, and PDAs are not only popular methods of communication, they're also ripe venues for bullying, often favored by girls, from upper elementary through high school. Cyber-bullying occurs when people are harassed, bullied, embarrassed, defamed, or pressured through electronic media. It can happen in e-mail exchanges, in chat rooms, in comment postings on blogs, and in the various constantly evolving social networking opportunities that are offered via the Internet.

Cyber-attacks and electronic bullying are quick to devise, easy to fire off, strike with ferocity, and can be copied to innumerable other observers, known and unknown, with astonishing speed and breadth. The tactics are constantly evolving, so keeping up with cyber-trends and technology is important for parents. This is why I encourage parents to get onto MySpace and visit chatrooms or blogs. You need to experience it in order to know how to talk to your kids about it. Be direct. Ask to see your child's MySpace or other personal site.

When we talk about cyber-bullying, the methods are a moving target, but they generally fall into one of these categories:

1. **Sending messages, often pretending to be someone else:** As Peggy discovered in the situation above, putting another child at risk is breathtakingly fast and easy. Predators prowl the Internet day and night in search of gullible and vulnerable kids. But this method is also used to bully others. Sending e-mails from an Internet café with a newly created screen name or e-mail address, a child can pretend to be anyone.

2. **Spreading malicious rumors or innuendoes:** Sending rumors in an e-mail, which can be forwarded with additional comments, is easy to do and hard to trace. This is a favored method of bullying and gets lots and lots of people involved. Using BCC (blind carbon copy) is another way that what appears to be a

communication between two people can be seen by an unlimited number of invisible voyeurs.

3. **Posting embarrassing photos and digital videos:** The introduction of cell phones with camera and video capacity has made this an increasing problem. Photos from gymnasiums, dressing rooms, bathrooms, and bedrooms are taken and sent with the click of a button.

4. **Sexual harassment:** Using photos, messages, or video, young people are harassing and embarrassing each other. Pop-ups, ads, and e-mails for "enhancement" and Internet drugs have become ubiquitous in the inboxes of most Internet users, and kids can sexually harass one another with the same materials. Central to addressing this problem is the need to educate kids about what sexual harassment is, why it is a form of bullying, and why it is illegal.

5. **Threats:** Scaring another person is also easy to do with the anonymity of electronic communication. Kids need to understand that this too is a form of bullying and that it is illegal.

6. **Stalking:** This is an increasing problem in romantic relationships. After a breakup, both boys and girls can become cyberstalkers. Rumors, false assertions, pictures, and videos can all come into play as one tries to ruin the reputation of the other. Civil rights legislation and the legal system may be slow to catch up with this trend, but their awareness is increasing and arrests are no longer uncommon.

Don't Let Your Child Become a Cyber-Bully

Q: *"My daughter has shown me a number of Internet pictures that show her classmates in unflattering situations. She has made a number of comments using the nicknames—all unkind—of kids who are not part of her social circle. At first, I admit, I sort of laughed with her, but then I began to really think about the impact this could have on the other girls as the images and nicknames are passed around the school. I'm not sure what to say now that I've already laughed at the nicknames and images."*

—Sandy R., *mother of fifteen-year-old*

SHERRYLL SAYS: *"We've all been there, laughing at something we knew to be unkind or bigoted. The best approach is the honest one. Tell your daughter, 'I know I laughed at the pictures and nicknames, but it has really bothered me since. I don't want to be an unkind person, and I don't want that for you, either. We need to take the higher road and refuse to participate in behavior that demeans others. We also need to set an example for others. So, I'm saying to you that this is not right, and I'd like you to consider giving the same message to your friends.' She may not change her behavior right away, but your opinion of her matters to her, and she will think about it over time. You should continue to look for opportunities to reinforce this message and try to shift her behavior over time."*

It is important to talk with your kids about cyber-bullying before it becomes a problem. Discuss how hurtful words can be, how written language can be just as vicious as spoken words, and how unkind gossip, rumors, and shared sniping are in any form. Setting family expectations, stating explicitly that unkindness, exploitation, and bullying are activities that will not be permitted, is critical.

Children often have things to say about events in their lives, conflicts with friends, or situations they become aware of. All of these are opportunities to discuss your family expectations, to let them know that they should not encourage or participate in this behavior. Be explicit about what you would expect of them if they become aware that others are involved in this behavior. Most kids know by third or fourth grade how fragile friendships can be. Just as they do not want to be the target of social bullying, they should not participate in it, even as an observer.

For example, young people frequently videotape themselves or others in compromising or abusive situations and post the videos on a site such as www.youtube.com. A quick e-mail lets everyone know the video is out there, and the situation then takes on a life of its own. This is both unethical and cruel. As you become aware of these incidents—and your kids may share them freely with you—take the opportunity to discuss how it would feel to be the target of something like this, and how it would feel to be responsible for perpetrating this abuse or allowing someone else to do so.

Just as elementary-school-age children need to learn empathy and think about how others feel, adolescents need to stay connected to how their behavior impacts others. For most teenagers, this is not the conversation they have with their friends; it is the conversation they need to have with their parents!

Protecting Your Kids from Internet Predators

Kids blog and spend time on social networking sites to "meet new friends." But this essentially anonymous communication makes it difficult to separate "new friends" from imposters. *Grooming* is the process by which sexual predators go from seemingly innocent communication to sexual exploitation. Grooming is manipulation that may look like flattery, sympathy, and offers of gifts, money, or jobs. It may take days or weeks, thus its name, "grooming." Grooming is quite personal and is designed to target the child's vulnerability. Anne Collier, on www.blogsafety.com, identifies some tactics kids can watch out for:

- "Let's go private." A suggestion to leave the public chatroom and create a private chat or move to instant messaging or telephone text messaging.
- "Where's your computer in the house?" Checking to see if parents might be around.
- "Who's your favorite band? Designer? Film? Gear?" Questions like these tell the groomer what gifts to offer (e.g., concert tickets, Webcam, software, clothes, CDs).
- "I know someone who can get you a modeling job." Flattery and appealing to a child's fantasies can be very effective.
- "I know a way you can earn money fast." One of the tactics that snagged Justin Berry, thirteen, into what became his Webcam prostitution business, as reported by the *New York Times*.
- "You seem sad. Tell me what's bothering you." The sympathy ploy can be very effective with alienated, depressed, or lonely young people.
- "What's your phone number?" Asking for personal information of any kind is a signal that should alert kids to terminate the conversation or let a parent know!
- "If you don't do what I ask, I'll tell your parents or post your photos." Intimidation is the most powerful lever of all. If children have already broken one of the rules, the fear of getting in even deeper trouble can cloud their judgment.

Five More Steps Parents Can Take

There are several other actions I recommend for parents, to keep track of what their children are being exposed to. These suggestions will be considered controversial by some—usually parents who haven't had to deal with the realities of technology predators, curious adolescents, and bullies. Each of us finds our own comfort zone with the issues of privacy and our children.

1. Use parental control software on your computers, your kids' computers, and your television.

2. Learn how to set and use the history feature on your Internet browser. Set it for the longest period possible and check it regularly. You really do want to know if your child is visiting porn or hate sites, or any other inappropriate sites. If you don't know what your child is being exposed to, you can't be part of the conversation about the risks.

3. If you have concerns about your children's activities, it is your right to check their e-mail and text messaging history in their cell phone or PDA, as well as whom they are calling or avoiding.

4. If you have concerns, check your children's rooms, pockets, backpacks, and so on. Kids are generally pretty unconscious about what they leave around, including notes from friends or bullies.

5. Check the cyber (and paper) magazines your kids frequent. Some teen magazines have moved into the range of soft porn and, again, you can't be part of the conversation if you haven't seen the materials.

TALK TO YOUR KIDS

- What if you are the subject of rumors or Internet gossip, but you don't want to get your friends in trouble or make things worse?

- What if you find out someone has posted embarrassing or revealing photos of you on the Internet, but you don't want us to know about it? What would you do? Is there anyone else you could tell?

- What if you have already given out information that you know you shouldn't have, or sent photos to someone?

- What if someone threatens you, or threatens to get you in trouble for something you've already done, if you don't do what he wants you to do? How would you handle that?
- What would you say to me if you were trying to get help with this situation?

Dealing with Unsafe Computer Usage

If your children disregard your rules for the computer, discuss the issues, and make sure that the consequences are logical and consistent. Steps might include:

1. Talk to your children explicitly about why your rules exist. Discuss the safety issues. Let your children know that their safety is important to you and that you take it seriously.
2. Be clear that communications over the Internet are actually with strangers—people that your children don't know, even if it seems that they do.
3. Explain that part of your job is keeping your children safe. If they ran out into the street when you let them go into the yard by themselves, you would stop letting them go out alone.
4. Likewise, if your children cannot follow the computer or electronic equipment rules, then electronic communication privileges go away for a set period of time.
5. Earning these privileges back should include a review of the rules, agreement to follow them, and a period of increased supervision. Your children should not be on the computer if you can't see clearly what they are viewing just by walking by.

Getting Schools Involved

Q: *"My son's school recently sent a letter to parents asking us to check our children's cell phones for indecent images of students. Apparently, there has been a series of incidents involving photos and videos of students being distributed, and they are trying to get them all erased, as well as asking us to talk with our children about this. Honestly, I feel it is an invasion of my son's privacy to go through his phone. How would you handle this?"*
                                    —James E., *parent of fourteen-year-old*

SHERRYLL SAYS: *"If you feel it is an invasion of his privacy, then I would share the letter with him, ask him to delete anything from his phone that he does not want you to see, and then check his phone. Whether you check his phone with his permission or knowledge or not, this is an opportunity to discuss the issues of privacy, electronic harassment, and the fact that what lives on his phone or PDA is readily viewable by others."*

In my conversations with school groups, it is apparent that this is a new problem for them, and many think that this type of bullying is harmless because it is not physical. But schools need to be an active part of this conversation. Effective programs have been developed to reduce bullying in schools. Research has found that bullying is most frequent in schools where there is poor adult supervision, where teachers and students ignore bullying behavior, and where rules against bullying are not consistently enforced.

DID YOU KNOW?

While approaches that simply crack down on individual bullies are seldom effective, when there is a schoolwide commitment to end bullying, it can be reduced by up to 50 percent. An effective program includes:

- Changing school and classroom climates
- Raising awareness about bullying
- Increasing teacher and parent involvement and supervision
- Forming clear rules and strong social norms against bullying
- Providing support and protection for all students.

If you become aware of an incident of cyber-bullying or harassment, bring it to the attention of your child's school immediately. You can help educate them regarding how vicious cyber-bullying can be once it is unleashed, explain why it should not be tolerated, and perhaps even help them set policies that protect everyone. With input and pressure from parents, schools will increasingly identify these behaviors as the cruel and thoughtless, sometimes illegal, behaviors that they are, rather than look away or even reinforce them by viewing them as clever, outrageous, or funny.

DAY 9: SUMMING IT UP

Cyber-safety requires ground rules and parental diligence! Parents need to understand the technology and the patterns of communication as they evolve. They also need to balance the evolving communication patterns of young people and safety concerns. Key points include:

- Keep computer equipment in a main living area.
- Discuss all aspects of cyber-safety with your children regularly.
- Don't prohibit Web access; monitor it.
- Set ground rules for usage and information sharing, and enforce them.
- Show an interest in your child's computer activities and know how to access the computer history, sites visited, and blogs.
- Keep up with advances in cyber-communication—your kids will show you how.
- Don't shy away from checking up on your child's communications if you sense a problem.
- Be open about cyber-abuse, what it is, and how easily traceable it is—everything leaves a signature.

Talk about cyber-bullying, what it is, how it feels, and why it is wrong. Forms of cyber-bullying to discuss include:

- Sending messages while pretending to be someone else
- Spreading rumors or using BCC (blind carbon copy) to open private communications to others
- Posting embarrassing photos or videos

- Sexual harassment
- Threats or stalking behaviors

The Internet is wide open and indispensable as a tool young people need to master, but that mastery requires boundaries and limits that are shaped and controlled by parents.

Advocating
for Others

Q: *"My daughter has shared with me a series of very disturbing incidents at her school. She has described other girls being very abusive toward a new girl who is from another part of the country. They have pinched her, kept her from the bathroom until she wet her pants, and made fun of her hair, her clothes, and her accent. My daughter clearly hasn't been part of this, but she is watching it go on."*

—Charlie O., *parent of fifth grader*

SHERRYLL SAYS: *"Your daughter should be acknowledged for speaking up about this situation. That is the first step in advocating for others. The discussion now should turn to how she can help. Her options should be determined by her comfort level. If she feels she can speak up directly to the bullying girls, she should practice with you, develop a plan, and then speak up on behalf of the targeted child. If she does not feel able to do that, you should develop a plan with her to let the school know so they are able to act."*

Bullying isn't invisible. Children often witness it, because it happens in the context of children being with one another. It happens in school buildings, in classrooms, on the playground, in homes, and in the neighborhood. Ask any child from kindergarten through high school who is bullying whom. The teacher may not be able to tell you, but the children all know—and they don't want to be next.

Being glad you're not the target is a natural response to witnessing bullying. But it is a response that is not very satisfying, and most children feel that they should be doing something. They hesitate because they don't really know what to do and because they don't want to become a target. These children are eager to learn what to do and how to intervene effectively. They are eager to become *advocates*, people who speak up for someone else.

To really change the nature of this problem, we need to shift the cultural norms that allow bullying and peer-to-peer abuse to continue.

Learning to Be an Advocate

Children who are neither bullies nor targets are the most powerful agents for change. They have the best social skills, the highest self-esteem, and the best conflict management resources. They are those most likely to be emulated, and they are more willing to assert themselves about differences without being aggressive or confrontational. They suggest compromises and alternate solutions. They tend to be more aware of people's feelings and are the children who can be most helpful in resolving disputes and assisting other children to get help.

Being an advocate for others is a powerful and rewarding thing to do. Depending on the ages of your children, ask them what an advocate is. Some kids know right away and understand the importance of advocates, but many don't. An advocate is someone who stands up for someone else. Being an advocate is about:

- Being a friend
- Being a good leader

- Helping one's home, school, and community to be places where people are treated with respect and kindness

As discussed throughout the book, bullies can be the outsiders, the kids who don't have very good social skills. They can be looking in from the outside of existing social circles. Advocates can let them know that their behavior is unacceptable and help them find more appropriate ways to be admitted to social circles. In essence, advocates can give them feedback on their negative behavior and offer a hand into the circle where people get along and treat each other with respect. For example, if there is a child in the classroom who constantly annoys others, your child might be able to take him aside and say, "It really bugs people when you do stuff like touching them as you go by or knocking stuff off their desk, and they don't want to be your friend. If you will try not to do that stuff, I will try to include you more in what we are doing. Can you do that?"

Social or relational bullies are more often the kids in the very center of social circles. These are the kids who have the power of social confidence and are successful and admired by many, including adults. While *Nineteen Minutes* by Jodi Picoult is a novel, her description of social bullies distills the essence of their actions and their sense of privilege:

It was not a surprise that someone had gotten into her e-mail account [and forwarded a private e-mail to the entire school]—they all knew each other's passwords; it could have been any of the girls. . . . But what would make her friends do something like this, something so totally humiliating? . . . [She] already knew the answer. This group of kids—they weren't her friends. Popular kids didn't really have friends; they had alliances. You were safe only as long as you hid your trust—at any moment someone might make you the laughingstock, because then they knew no one was laughing at them.

When the young woman in *Nineteen Minutes* tries to stand up to the bully, saying, "I don't like the way you treat kids who aren't like us, all right? Just because you don't want to hang out with losers doesn't mean you have to torture them, does it?" His response sums it all up: "Yeah, it does. . . . Because if there isn't a *them*, there can't be an *us*."

In a case like this, the bully is at the center of the social circle, surrounded by friends and peers. In the next circle out are admirers and kids who hope to stay out of the bully's view, those who are afraid they might be targeted. The next outer circle includes the kids who are ignored, belittled, dismissed, or directly targeted by the bully and his or her friends. The greatest opportunity to give feedback, to reshape the bully's behavior, or to advocate for others lies with the kids in the second circle. This takes courage, but it can be done.

How to Be an Advocate

Learning to be an advocate includes all of the skills your kids have learned through the course of this book. It includes recognizing bullying, having empathy for the target, and being able to communicate effectively and assertively about the bullying behavior.

Kids who are advocates generally have better social skills and conflict management skills than either bullies or targets. They are more willing to assert themselves about differences without being aggressive or confrontational. They suggest compromises and alternate solutions. They tend to be more aware of people's feelings and are the children who can be most helpful in resolving disputes and assisting other children to get help. Teaching this group of children that bullying is unacceptable and giving them the skills to be advocates, to intervene immediately and consistently, is how we can create the possibility of reducing the levels of bullying in this culture.

Three Big Messages

Through the role-play below, you will see the process of being an advocate. But the three primary messages children want to communicate as advocates are:

1. Bullying behavior is unacceptable in this community (school, house, and neighborhood).
2. We do not want to be around people who treat others with disrespect.
3. We are going to report bullying that is ongoing, that we are unable to stop through our own efforts.

Role-playing to teach your child how to be an advocate is one of the most surprising and enjoyable parts of the Take a Stand Program. I am constantly amazed at the willingness of children to step forward on behalf of others, once they have the confidence and know how to do it well. Practice these role-plays, as well as those your child may think of. Discuss how these skills might be applicable in your child's school or circle of friends.

> **ROLE-PLAY:** *Temper Tantrum*
> Ask your child, "What if your friend has a little temper tantrum every time he doesn't do well on the field? Other kids are starting to make fun of him. What could you say and do?"
> **ACTION 1:** Role-play taking him aside and telling him he's making himself look silly. Suggest another way to deal with his frustration.
> **ACTION 2:** Role-play talking to your teacher and telling

him about the playground behavior. Ask the teacher if the class could talk about good sportsmanship so everyone could learn to get along better.

ROLE-PLAY: *Crying Child*

Ask, "What if a bully said to another child, 'You're so stupid, you'll never get to second grade.' Pretend that the first grader doesn't know what to do or starts to cry. What could you do as an advocate?"

ACTION 1: Walk up to the bully, look him in the eye, stand up tall, and say clearly and firmly, "Don't do that; that's not nice." Then take the first grader's hand and walk away.

ACTION 2: Get a friend to go with you to confront the bully, saying, "We don't treat people that way in our school." Then take the first grader to play with your group of friends.

ROLE-PLAY: *Can I Play?*

Ask, "What if you and your friends are playing, and another girl walks up and asks to play? One of your friends says she can't. What would you do as an advocate?"

ACTION 1: Speak up and say, "That's not very nice; let's invite her to play."

ACTION 2: Speak up and say, "I think we hurt her feelings. I'm going to play with her." Then leave the group to play with her.

ROLE-PLAY: *Pushed Around*

Ask, "What if you see three or four other kids poking and pushing a new kid around? What could you say or do as an advocate?"

ACTION 1: Say, "Picking on other people isn't nice." Then leave with the targeted child.

ACTION 2: Say, "Why would we want to play with kids who are mean?" Then go do something else with the bullied child.

As you role-play, you'll want to again talk about empathy, so kids clearly understand what it is and why it matters. Remind your child what it feels like to be excluded, what it feels like to see someone else being excluded, and what it feels like to stand up, to be an advocate for someone else. How would your child feel if s/he was being bullied and a friend jumped in to help?

As this conversation develops, you will find the middle ground in which nice kids behave thoughtlessly or bully to protect another relationship they value. For example, say one of your daughter's friends starts to be mean to her because your daughter is spending time with a new friend. This is an opportunity to discuss what is happening, and for your daughter to respond directly to the behavior. She might say, "You are still my friend, but I don't like it when you are mean to me because I also like other people."

TALK WITH YOUR KIDS

- Have you ever witnessed bullying and wanted to do something about it?
- Have you hesitated because you were afraid the bully would turn on you?
- Have you ever tried to stop bullying? What happened?
- Have you ever seen someone else successfully stop bullying? What happened?
- Would you like to learn how to stop bullying?

This feedback is important in relationships. It enables kids to work out a problem, to state that bullying and mean behavior are unacceptable, and to continue to be friends. For the jealous, bullying child, it signals a need to find better ways to deal with her feelings and lets her know that she jeopardizes the relationships she values when she behaves like a bully.

ROLE-PLAY: *Name-Calling*
Ask, "What if a bully is pushing a kid around and calling him names? The kid says, 'Don't make fun of me, it isn't nice and I don't like it,' but the bully continues. What would you say and do?"

ACTION 1: Say, "Stop it; we're not going to put up with that in our school."

ACTION 2: Say, "If you don't stop, I am going to take him to the teacher, and she can deal with your bullying!" Then leave with the bullied child.

ROLE-PLAY: *Group Games*
Ask, "What if a new friend of yours wants to join your group game? One of your old friends says, 'You're a loser and you can't be a part of this game.' How would you respond?"

ACTION 1: Say, "You guys know better than that. Give her a chance; she might be a great player."

DISCUSSION: How does it feel to be an advocate versus being part of the crowd? Is it harder to stand up for someone when the bullying is being done by people you like? Does advocacy look different when the bullies are your friends?

How to Ask for Help

One of the most important things an advocate can do is notify adults and ask for help. Again, a distinction must be made between tattling and being a responsible student citizen. Asking for help is not tattling, and advocates should always find a way to go beyond what they can do themselves, if it is needed. Brainstorm with your child ways in which s/he could ask for help. It might be with an anonymous letter to the principal. It might be with a confidential meeting with a school counselor. It might be by bringing it up in a classroom meeting. Whatever the method, advocates are in the best position to recognize when bullying has reached a level that requires adult intervention and then to seek it!

ROLE-PLAY: *Held Back*
Ask, "What if you see a bully taunting another kid, saying, 'You got held back; you must be stupid!' What could you say and do?"
ACTION 1: Say, "Cut it out; you don't need to make yourself feel bigger by being mean to someone else."
ACTION 2: Say, "That is mean and you can't say that!" Then take the bullied child away from the area.
ACTION 3: Tell a teacher about what is happening.

ROLE-PLAY: *Nasty Rumors*
Ask, "What if kids are making up rumors and calling a girl names, saying she is a slut, or worse? She is being ostracized in the lunchroom, before and after school. Some of this is being done by your friends. What would you say or do?"
ACTION 1: Say, "She may not be one of our friends, but this is just mean. We need to stop it!"
ACTION 2: Say, "It is not okay to make someone feel this bad. I don't want any part of this."

DISCUSSION: Would it be hard to go up against your friends like this? If it feels impossible to even deal with a situation like this, what else could you do? Is there a counselor or teacher who would help? Would you be willing to back away from your friends for a while over an issue like this? Why, or why not?

A role-play like this gets to the heart of the power of social groups in middle and high school. Remember that bullying hits its peak in middle school, which is also a time when kids are trying to find a group where they fit in. This is profoundly difficult for kids, and the importance of advocacy should be part of any discussion with kids in this age group.

Parents as Advocates

Q: *"My daughter is a ten-year-old, tall, aggressive athlete. Last year she was pushed down at practice by a girl thirty pounds heavier than she, who wanted to catch the kickball which was coming at my daughter. This same girl pushed another girl down last week and then stood over her (she still had the ball in her hands), screaming, 'Give me the ball!' She pushed another girl into the wall because she couldn't get past her on the way to the lockers. The community center continues to 'investigate.' I shouldn't have to take my daughter out of sports because they refuse to handle this kid."*

—Jacque J., *parent of ten-year-old*

SHERRYLL SAYS: *"This is a situation that should have been handled by the coach or the community center long before now. Since they are not recognizing the severity of the problem, your options are to get other parents involved to demand that the community center*

> *address the problem and suspend the aggressor from play as a
> consequence, or to notify the supervisors of the parent organiza-
> tion to demand action. This is not uncommon in kid sports, but
> it needs to be addressed more frequently to protect other players
> and to get help for the aggressor."*

Jacque's child isn't the only one in trouble here—her community
center is in denial. This is a child who will continue to escalate
her aggressive behaviors without intervention. A school or youth
organization cannot be safe for anyone if the appropriate authori-
ties can't respond to dangerous situations like this. And these are
the very places we need our kids to feel safe.

Based on the hundreds of e-mails I receive every year, dealing
with an unresponsive organization is a frustrating experience for
many families. Often an "investigation" lags, not because schools
and communities don't recognize the problem, but because they
don't know how to address it effectively. Bullying needs to be
identified for what it is—abusive behavior. It needs to be dealt with
clearly, firmly, and consistently. In a case such as this, suspension
should be the consequence. Kids who cannot participate in sports
with respect for others shouldn't be allowed to play.

Steps That Schools Need To Take

If you are engaged in a conversation about bullying with your
child's school, you should know that there are clearly defined steps
schools can take to deal with current bullying and reduce future
bullying. The first step is acknowledging that bullying is a problem
in the school. The second step is developing a clear and simple
policy. This includes setting clear ground rules and expectations
for behavior, establishing consequences for breaking the rules,
and then—the hard part—following through consistently.

Children who are bullies need to be dealt with consistently and
effectively. Bullying should never be overlooked or excused. This

only adds to the problem. Bullying gives kids an experience of power that, left unchecked, builds on itself. Without intervention, bullying behavior continues and the bullying activities escalate in severity as children get older.

When bullying is reported at school, it is not important at that moment why the bullying occurred. The discussion with a bullying child should focus on several key points:

- Bullying is not acceptable in our school, family, or society.
- If you are feeling frustrated, angry, or aggressive, here are some things you can do (teachers, counselors, or administrators should provide concrete examples based on the current situation).
- Schools need to help young people role-play or act out the new behaviors, so the child can experience a new response. Schools also need to remember that role-play is the key to changing behavior!
- School counselors may ask, "How can I help you address your anger or upset?" They can help children develop a plan for getting help when they find themselves getting into this type of situation again.
- Schools need to specify concretely the consequences of the aggression or bullying and impose them.
- Schools should establish some form of "restorative justice" to give the child a way to heal the damage inflicted on the targeted child or the community as a whole.
- The objective is to stop the behavior, give the child better skills to address his or her feelings, then teach and reward more appropriate behavior.

Schools, just like parents, need to remember that bullying is about power and control. They need to look for ways to shut down the child's bullying power and boost his or her ability to be a contributing member of the community. They need to help children find a way to feel part of the community, and give each child a way to contribute to the community. For example, a bully might be put in charge of a project to help educate peers about conflict resolution strategies. A bully could be paired up with a coach to manage the equipment in the gym. A bully might take the lead in developing a restorative justice panel where other children who have been bullies have an opportunity to find a way to contribute to the school community rather than being destructive to it.

This is an area where parents can and should be involved. In addition to participating in classroom activities, many parents willingly volunteer to help monitor the lunchroom, or the playgrounds before and after school. Parents should be a part of policy-making meetings so they have input on how bullying affects the community.

Just as role-play is the key to developing skills for kids, any schoolwide initiative to prevent bullying must have many action components. Putting posters in the classrooms and holding an assembly may make schools feel that they are addressing the problem. In reality, however, it may be worse than doing nothing, because children may get the message that the school knows there is a problem with bullying and isn't really doing anything effective to stop it.

DID YOU KNOW?

Bullying can follow people into the workplace, but studies find that bullying bosses differ in significant ways from the bullies of childhood.

In the schoolyard, particularly among elementary-school boys, bullies tend to pick on smaller or weaker children, often to assert control in an uncertain social environment in which the bullies feel vulnerable. But adult bullies in positions of power are already dominant, and they are just as likely to pick on a strong subordinate as a weak one.

Women are at least as likely as men to be the aggressors, and they are more likely to be targets.

Elements of School Programs That Work

Programs that work need several elements:

1. Assessment of the level of the problem
2. Policy regarding education about bullying and response to bullying
3. Educational plan for every grade, every year, including professional staff, parents, and all children
4. Educational program that includes:
   - Identification of the problem in all its forms
   - Development of understanding of the impact of bullying on all children
   - Role-play to develop skills for preventing bullying, as well as intervention when bullying occurs
   - Development of an advocacy approach whereby all children take responsibility for bullying that occurs in the school
   - Clear and consistent consequences for bullying, including a restorative justice plan
5. Evaluation of program effectiveness

The Power for Social Change

The cycle of bullying, where targets become bullies who create more targets and more bullies, can only be changed with the participation of all of us. As parents, we can train our children to be more empathic, more assertive, and more willing to speak up for others. We can recognize bullying when it occurs and act on behalf of bullies and their targets. We can demand that schools stop tolerating bullying and interpersonal violence. We can create a culture that no longer looks away when children are shunned or tormented or made to feel worthless.

If each of us does that, if each of us takes responsibility for speaking up for each child in our sphere of influence, we can save lives. We can prevent another generation of children who are belittled and abused. We can prevent future Columbines. We can move in the direction of a world that respects each person as we should respect ourselves.

DAY 10: SUMMING IT UP

Bullying isn't invisible; kids see it happening every day. Those who are neither the bullies nor the targets don't act because:

- They don't know what to say or do.
- They are afraid they will be the next target.
- They don't believe adults will do anything to help.

Most children have a keen sense of right and wrong and are willing to act if they know how. Teaching kids to be advocates gives them the ability to intervene effectively on behalf of other children. It enables them to communicate to the bully and to others in their circle of peers that:

- Bullying is an unacceptable behavior.
- It is not all right to treat others with disrespect.
- Bullying will be reported and stopped.

In this, and all other areas discussed in this book, these concepts and skills are best taught through role-play, actually using the skills in real-life situations, and then talking about what happened, what worked, what didn't. It is this process that builds our children's capacity to assess social situations, to make choices, and to take action that nurtures and supports all the individuals in their community.

RESOURCES

Books for Adults

Carson, Richard. *Taming Your Gremlin: A Guide to Enjoying Yourself.* New York, NY: Harper Perennial, 1983.
This is my favorite book for grownups, to inform the parenting of our children. It is an entertaining, creative, and powerful approach to identifying the narrator in your head, the positive and negative roles it plays, and how to use it to create a happier, more fulfilling, and satisfying life.

Dawson, Geraldine, Sally Ozonoff, and James McPartland. *A Parent's Guide to Asperger Syndrome and High-Functioning Autism: How to Meet the Challenges and Help Your Child Thrive.* New York, NY: Guilford Press, 2002.
Children and teens with these disorders often stand out for their precocious intelligence and language abilities—yet profound social difficulties can limit every aspect of their lives. This hopeful, compassionate guide shows parents how to work with their child's unique impairments and capabilities to help their child learn to engage more fully with the world and live as self-sufficiently as possible.

Espeland, Pamela. *Knowing Me, Knowing You: The I-Sight Way to Understand Yourself and Others.* Minneapolis, MN: Free Spirit Publishing, 2001.

This book is very valuable for helping families to discover their personal style. It brings to light how young people think, how they respond under stress, and what frustrates and angers them. With this understanding, individuals and families can find harmony and respect to embrace and build upon their differences as well as their similarities.

Friedman, Thomas. *The World Is Flat: A Brief History of the Twenty-First Century.* New York, NY: Farrar, Straus and Giroux, 2005.

While the geography of our planet hasn't changed, Friedman shows how globalization is resulting in a new world economy where the playing field for all the children of the world will become increasingly equalized because of technology.

Heck, Tom. "Team Activities on a Shoestring." 2006. Available online at www.teachmeteamwork.com.

A wonderful free e-book containing eight teambuilding games that really work to help kids learn cooperative problem solving with just two shoestrings!

Horn, Sam. *Tongue Fu!: How to Deflect, Disarm, and Defuse Any Verbal Conflict.* New York, NY: St. Martin's Griffin, 1997, and *Tongue Fu! at School: 30 Ways to Get Along Better with Teachers, Principals, Students, and Parents.* Lanham, MD: Taylor Trade Publishing, 2004.

These books are filled with practical tips and tools to help kids learn communication skills, including focusing on solutions, persuading others to stop and listen, handling hassles with humor, keeping emotions under control, and turning resentment into rapport.

Magid, Larry, and Collier, Anne. *MySpace Unraveled: A Parent's Guide to Teen Social Networking.* Berkeley, CA: Peachpit Press, 2006.

Between this book and the Web site www.blogsafety.com,

Magid and Collier help parents understand the social networking phenomenon and provide step-by-step instructions on how to keep their young and savvy producers, socializers, and uploaders safe. See www.myspaceunraveled.com.

Moyes, Rebecca and Susan Moreno. *Incorporating Social Goals in the Classroom: A Guide for Teachers and Parents of Children with High-Functioning Autism and Asperger Syndrome.* Philadelphia, PA: Jessica Kingsley Publishers, 2001.

This book provides practical, hands-on strategies to teach social skills to children with high-functioning autism and Asperger syndrome. It includes a detailed description of the social deficits of these children as they appear in the classroom—difficulties with such things as understanding idioms, taking turns in conversation, understanding and using tone of voice and body language—and ways to address them.

Paley, Vivian Gussin. *You Can't Say You Can't Play.* Cambridge, MA: Harvard University Press, 1992.

Vivian Paley explores and challenges the commonly accepted practice of letting children exclude each other, showing how socially dominant children use exclusion as a tool to enforce their dominance. She explores negative consequences for the group as a whole and proposes a solution that is about building a culture of tolerance and problem solving in kindergarten.

Books for Kids

Agassi, Martine. *Hands Are Not for Hitting.* Minneapolis, MN: Free Spirit Publishing, 2000.

This gentle, encouraging book helps young children understand that hands are for saying hello, for playing, sharing, clapping, counting, helping, building things, being kind, and staying safe. Simple words and inviting illustrations reinforce two main themes: violence is never okay, and every child is capable of positive, loving actions. For kindergarten and early elementary aged children.

———. *Hands Are Not for Hitting*. Minneapolis, MN: Free Spirit Publishing, 2002.

This hardcover book by the same name as the kindergarten and early elementary version, is a Parent's Choice award-winning picture book appropriate for preschoolers. It's never too early to learn about the many good things hands can do. Simple words and charming pictures invite even the youngest children to use their hands for fun and caring actions, and to understand that hitting is never okay.

Chessen, Sherri. *Gorp's Dream: A Tale of Diversity, Tolerance, and Love in Pumpernickel Park*. Phoenix, AZ: The Gorp Group, 2003.

Gorp was born to be a symbol for all things good and nonviolent. He helps children learn lessons like respect and responsibility, while being loving, kind, friendly, and fair. With fanciful and interesting illustrations, this book explores bullying and teasing. It teaches that everyone can get along, including tortillas, bagels, cookies, sourdough bread, and English muffins. Appropriate for first through third graders.

Cosby, Bill. *Meanest Thing to Say*. New York, NY: Scholastic Books, 1997.

This is a Little Bill book for beginning readers. To win the game, Little Bill must say mean things to the new boy. But wait! Can Little Bill be a winner and a nice person? Written by Bill Cosby, Little Bill books affirm the value of friendships and family relationships, and encourage children to solve problems fairly and creatively. This book features a letter to parents by child psychiatry specialist Dr. Alvin Poussaint. This softcover book is appropriate for first- or second-grade readers or as a read-aloud.

Crawford, Judy A. *Doogie Dinosaur Learns a Lesson.* Alberta, Canada: Just Judy Publishing, 2003.

D&D is a mean, green, bully dinosaur, who comes to town and is putting everyone down. This picture book, appropriate for preschool and kindergarten, simply and clearly gives children experience of what it feels like to be a bully and to be the target of bullying. It models how to make friends and get along.

McCain, Becky Ray. *Nobody Knew What to Do: A Story about Bullying.* Morton Grove, IL: Albert Whitman & Co., 2001.

This is the story of a new boy in school, who is spat on when the teacher's not looking. The bullies are successful, and the new boy doesn't want to come to school anymore. But one boy steps up and asks for help from the classroom teacher. Together, this group of children discovers how to end bullying in their school.

Paley, Vivian Gussin. *Girl with the Brown Crayon.* Cambridge, MA: Harvard University Press, 1998.

Reeny, one of Ms. Paley's most outgoing students, has established a kinship with Fredrick, a fictional mouse in a Leo Lionni book. Using this information, Ms. Paley develops her kindergarten curriculum around books written by Leo Lionni to explore issues of gender, age, and racism.

Perez, L. King. *First Day in Grapes.* New York, NY: Lee and Low Books, 2002.

All year long, Chico and his family move up and down the state of California picking fruits and vegetables. Every September, they pick grapes, and every year Chico starts at a new school again. Often, other people pick on him, maybe because he's new, or maybe because he speaks Spanish.

When Chico goes to fourth grade, the bullies confront him
in the lunchroom. Readers of all backgrounds will relate to
Chico's bravery in the creative way he finds to resolve the
conflict. This is a story of inner strength and community.
Appropriate for third through fifth graders.

Romain, Trevor. *Cliques, Phonies, & Other Baloney.* Minneapolis,
MN: Free Spirit Publishing, 1988.

A straightforward, entertaining discussion of what really
goes on in social groups.

Verdick, Elizabeth. *Teeth Are Not For Biting.* Minneapolis, MN:
Free Spirit Publishing, 2003.

Sooner or later, almost all young children bite someone.
Teeth Are Not for Biting tells the truth about teeth: Ouch!
Biting hurts. Simple words and charming pictures invite
even the youngest child to discover better ways to cope with
frustration. It includes helpful hints for parents and caregivers. Hardcover, appropriate for preschoolers.

———. *Words Are Not For Hurting.* Minneapolis, MN: Free Spirit
Publishing, 2004.

Some words are loud, and some are soft. Some are kind,
some are not. Even very young children can learn the difference. They can be responsible for what they say, and
they can choose words that are helpful, not hurtful. This
book shows them how. Simple words and charming pictures teach little ones big ideas. Hardcover, appropriate for
preschoolers.

Webster-Doyle, Terrence. *Why Is Everybody Always Picking On
Me: A Guide to Handling Bullies.* New York, NY: Weatherhill,
1991.

This book is for young people who have been bullied and
want to understand the problem and deal with it creatively.
This book is also for young people who bully others. It
is filled with interesting and provocative illustrations,

thought-provoking exercises, opportunities to solve problems and role-play, and suggestions for adults. Appropriate for upper elementary and middle school.

References and Statistical Links

American Academy of Child and Adolescent Psychiatry. "Helping Teenagers with Stress." Facts for Families No. 66, 2005. Available online at http://www.aacap.org/page.ww?section=Facts+for+Families&name=Helping+Teenagers+With+Stress.

Asidao Christine S., Shontelle Vion, and Dorothy Espelage. "Interviews with Middle School Students: Bullying Victimization and Contextual Factors." *Journal of Emotional Abuse* (2001)

Batsche, G. M., and H. M. Knoff. "Bullies and their victims: Understanding a pervasive problem in the schools." *School Psychology Review* 23, no. 2 (1994): 165–174.

BlogSafety.com: Smart Socializing Starts Here, www.blogsafety.com.

Brotherson, Sean. "Understanding Brain Development in Young Children." Fargo, ND: North Dakota State University Extension Service, FS-609, April, 2005. Available online at http://www.ag.ndsu.edu/pubs/yf/famsci/fs609w.htm.

Clark, A. J. "Communication confidence and listening competence: An investigation of the relationships of willingness to communicate, communication apprehension and receiver apprehension to comprehension of content and emotional meaning in spoken messages." *Communication Education* 38, no. 3 (1989): 237–249.

Daro, Deborah. "Prevention, Replicating Child Abuse Prevention Programs: A Word of Caution." *The APSAC Advisor* (Spring 1991).

Finkelhor, David and Jennifer Dzuiba-Leatherman. "Victimization Prevention Programs: A National Survey of Children's Exposure and Reactions." *Child Abuse & Neglect* 19, no. 2 (1995): 129–139.

Fryer, George E., Sherryll Kraizer, and Thomas Miyoshi. "Measuring Actual Reduction of Risk to Child Abuse: A New Approach." *Child Abuse and Neglect* 11, no. 2 (1987): 173–179.

Fryer, George E., Sherryll Kraizer, and Thomas Miyoshi. "Measuring Children's Retention of Skills to Resist Stranger Abduction: Use of the Simulation Technique." *Child Abuse and Neglect,* Volume 11, no. 2 (1987): 181–185.

Hoover, J. H., R. Oliver, R. J. Hazler. "Bullying: perceptions of adolescent victims in the Midwestern USA." *School Psychology International* 13 (1992): 5–16.

Kraizer, Sherryll, Susan S. Witte, and George E. Fryer, Jr. "Child Sexual Abuse Prevention Programs: What Makes Them Effective in Protecting Children." *Children Today* (September-October, 1989).

Kraizer, Sherryll, George E. Fryer, and Marilyn Miller. "Programming for Preventing Sexual Abuse and Abduction: What Does It Mean When It Works?" *Child Welfare: Journal of the Child Welfare League of America, Inc.* (January-February 1988).

Kraizer, Sherryll, "Rethinking Prevention." *Child Abuse and Neglect* 10, no. 22 (1986): 259–261.

Loescher, Liz. "Cooling Off Thoughts" adapted from The Conflict Center, Denver, Colorado, www.conflictcenter.org.

Mehrabian, A. *Silent messages: Implicit communication of emotions and attitudes.* Belmont, CA: Wadsworth, 1981.

Meisels, Atkins-Burnett, and Nicholson, National Center for Educational Statistics. Available at: http://nces.ed.gov/

Namie, Gary. "What Makes a Boss a Bully?" *Management Issue*

News, June 22, 2004. See also Workplace Bullying and Trauma Institute, www.bullyinginstitute.org/.

Nansel, T. R., M. Overpeck, R. S. Pilla, W. J. Ruan, B. Simons-Morton, and P. Scheidt. "Bullying Behaviors among US Youth: Prevalence and Association with Psychosocial Adjustment." *Journal of the American Medical Association* 285, no. 16 (2001): 2094–2100.

National Women's Health Information Center, U.S. Department of Health and Human Services. See www.GirlsHealth.gov.

Oliver, R., J. H. Hoover, and R. Hazler. "The perceived roles of bullying in small-town Midwestern schools." *Journal of Counseling and Development* 72, no. 4 (1994): 416–419.

Olweus, D., S. Limber, and S. Mihalic. *Blueprints for Violence Prevention, Book Nine: Bullying Prevention Program.* Boulder, CO: Center for the Study and Prevention of Violence, 1999.

Olweus, D. *Bullying At School: What We Know and What We Can Do.* Cambridge, MA: Blackwell Publishers, Inc., 1993.

Picoult, Jodi. *Nineteen Minutes.* New York, NY: Atria Books, 2007, 218, 318.

U.S. Department of Education, National Center for Education Statistics, National Household Education Survey, 1993. *Student Victimization At School.* Results of a nationwide survey given in 1993 to students in sixth through twelfth grade. Available online at http://nces.ed.gov/pubs95/web/95204.asp.

Zarzour, Kim. *Schoolyard Bully.* Toronto, Canada: Harper Collins, 1999.

INDEX